Letters from Annapolis

Washington, D. C., Oct. 27th, 1848.

Brother John,

I have just returned from the Secretary's office. You cannot imagine what a straight I have gone through. So far all is well. (Excuse bad writing for I am in such a state I can ~~write~~ scarcely write at all.) I thought once or twice that I would have to return home, but I shall not do that. The Secretary asked me how old I was, to which I promptly replied. He read to me the regulations (not laws) about these matters; he then said it was against the regulation to admit any into the service over seventeen,—called up a Chief Clerk, and told him to give me orders in my name, which he did,—and which I have in my possession. When I was taking leave of Mason I could say no more than "Good Morning,"—but he understood my feelings, and I was satisfied. My appointment is to report tomorrow, or as shortly thereafter as possible. I shall wait, and study another week—then, one more trial, and I will be through! I will return to Annapolis in the evening train (I came up yesterday evening) and study hard. The examination is a small affair. I have been all through the Capitol,—saw the paintings in the Rotunda, and that vacant panel which, if I was able, I would rather fill with a design of my own, than be President. I shall visit the National Institute and Navy Yard before I leave, if I can. I came up from the junction of the Railroad with Mr. Upshur, a clerk in the Navy Department,—a nephew of the Captain and the Secretary who was killed on board the Princeton, down in the Potomac river. The three days I was in Annapolis I studied part at St. John's and some at my boarding house. I was in the Senate chamber, and saw Sully's picture of Carrollton, and Judge somebody!—and I stood on the spot where Washington resigned his commission to the Continental Congress, in the Old State House of Maryland, built before the Revolution. I have now about twelve dollars in my purse, but I can get a complete set of uniforms with far less than my traveling expenses, which will be ten cents per mile—83 dollars in all. I intended visiting the President, but I shall not stay until to-night—this is his evening to receive visitors. At 4 o'clock I shall make start back to Annapolis. You must direct your letters there. I have been in some anxiety for about a week, but I have taken everything easy. Write to me soon. I am now stopping at the Willard House. I stopped at the Eutaw House in Baltimore. I always stop at the best houses wherever I go. This letter is about me, myself,—very full of "I"—hope the next will be more interesting.

Your brother

W. P. McCann.

Letters from Annapolis

Midshipmen Write Home, 1848–1969

Edited by Anne Marie Drew

Naval Institute Press   Annapolis, Maryland

Library of Congress Cataloging-in-Publication Data
Letters from Annapolis : midshipmen write home, 1848–1969 /
[edited by] Anne Marie Drew.
p. cm.
Includes index.
ISBN 1-55750-170-X (alk. paper)
1. United States Naval Academy—Students—Correspondence.
2. Military cadets—Maryland—Annapolis—Correspondence.
3. Midshipmen—Maryland—Annapolis—Correspondence.
4. Annapolis (Md.)—Biography.
V415.M1A4 1998
359'.0071'173—dc21 98-4956

Printed in the United States of America on acid-free paper ♾
05 04 03 02 01 00 99 98 9 8 7 6 5 4 3 2
First printing

To Tony,
who has always understood the importance of God, flag, country, and J.P.J.

Contents

Acknowledgments

My first debt is to my U.S. Naval Academy (USNA) colleagues, past and present, who challenge, inspire, provoke, and entertain me. The prolific diversity of the USNA English Department attracted me from my very first day on the Yard. I consider myself lucky to exist among such people. Special thanks to Mike Parker, who generously gave me the idea for this book; to Charlie Nolan, who has provided support of every important kind; to Allyson, who could not be a better friend.

To the Masqueraders, I owe a particular debt. Since 1991, my work with this ever-changing group of midshipmen has deepened my love and respect for the Naval Academy. Everyone from the stump carrier to the executioner who used that stump to behead Sir Thomas More has become an important part of my work here. The special ones know who they are, and they understand that even though life circumstances will change, I will cherish their memories and keep their spirits alive in Mahan Hall.

The academy granted me a sabbatical in the spring of 1997, allowing me time to finish *Letters from Annapolis.*

Bill Cogar provided invaluable help—quite simply—because he knows so much. He tacitly reminded me that these letters represent more than the adolescent outpourings of boys writing home to their concerned mothers. Again and again, he'd nudge me in the direction of an historical source that proved useful. His interest in the project provided encouragement when the task seemed an overwhelming one.

The Special Collections and Archives staff at Nimitz Library offered unique help. Beverly Lyall, Mary Rose Catalfano, and especially Alice S. Creighton guided me through the primary sources that are here transcribed. Gary Lavalley, in his first week at USNA, helped to locate photographs. With patient good nature, the staff abided my comings and goings, my appearances and disappearances. Alice S. Creighton, who must be one of the most gracious people ever created, taught me much of what I know about academy history, simply by talking to me. In addition to the professional expertise of the library staff, I came to rely on their good company as a welcome relief from the sometimes tedious task of transcribing these letters.

Gerry Motl, the Reverend Mason Shambach, and Sister Mary Charles Weschler added a depth to this collection that might otherwise be absent. Gerry and Mason sent me photos and clippings to give me a fuller view of their lives at USNA. In numerous phone conversations their memories of the academy during the 1960s and 1970s proved helpful. Sister Mary Charles made me realize the importance of publishing these letters. Her brother Charles sacrificed everything—home, a new wife, a new baby, and ultimately his life—for his country in World War II. That ultimate sacrifice, the potential fate of every midshipman, deserves repeated recognition.

Like Bottom in *A Midsummer Night's Dream,* Ty volunteered to play any part necessary to help me finish this manuscript on time. He played multiple roles, from proofreader to cheerleader. No one has been kinder.

And finally, there are "the five Drews," who in 1990 moved with me to Maryland. I am grateful that they came, even though they could not stay.

Introduction

"I won't write in a diary or journal," Charles Weschler told his mother when he left for the academy in 1928, "but I'll write home and you can keep my letters." And Charles did write home, regularly. When the mail arrived at the Weschler home in Erie, Pennsylvania, his mother read the letters aloud to the family. Then the neatly handwritten letters were placed on a small shelf near the kitchen sink, and anyone was free to reread them. Not wanting to miss her mother's readings, eight-year-old Marion Weschler, Charles's little sister, made sure she was home when the mail arrived. The letters became a family treasure, especially after Charles died as a Japanese prisoner of war in 1945.

Someone, somewhere kept each collection of letters contained in this volume. The letters provide a firsthand account of midshipman life from 1848 through 1969. Writing to his mother in 1859, for example, Oliver Ambrose Batcheller attempted to provide her with a look at his new life. "You would like to see me in my uniform. Brass buttons enough to sink a person should he fall overboard." Like the other midshipmen whose correspondence comprises *Letters from Annapolis,* Batcheller supplied specific details about academy life and routine: "As for eating I can find no fault . . . for there is enough of it and that pretty good . . . the one with the longest arm fares the best."

In trying to capture for their friends and family the spirit and routine of the academy, the midshipmen often drew little pictures, quoted their classmates, poked fun at their professors. When the academy changed the style of the uniform cap in 1877, Harry Phelps wrote home to express the student dislike of the new design. Sketching a simple pen and ink drawing of the new design, Phelps complained humorously about the new look: "It looks just like a policeman's cap only it has an anchor instead of a number. . . . There is hardly an officer here that likes the proposed style of cap. One of them wants it [because] he is bald on top of his head . . . and he wants a cap which can . . . cover the bald spot."

While providing varying degrees of insight into the universal elements of academy life—grades, formation, drill, demerits, homesickness—the letters also provide a unique picture of American history, written from the firsthand perspective of those who were a part of it. As the country sat on the verge of the Civil War, Philip Henry Cooper described the political turmoil to his parents: "The southerners are determined that Lincoln shall not be inaugurated and it is rumored that there is a secret organization . . . to shoot Lincoln."

After participating in President Wilson's inauguration, Ellsworth Davis wrote to his father on March 5, 1913: "Then we marched off to the Capitol where we lined up in columns of companies facing the corps. We were very near the President's stand but could not hear what he said." In 1918, as the influenza epidemic swept the country, Orin Haskell's letters show the alarm and outrage that many in the country felt: "Perhaps you have heard that the influenza has us here. We have 1000 cases and four deaths so far." He added, "And they say the Germans introduced the disease. . . . This is one more thing to hate them for. I did not hate the German people at the beginning of the war but certainly do now and if I ever get a chance to kill a German, I shall kill him good." Shortly after the assassination of Martin Luther King Jr., Midshipman Barry Shambach wrote home to explain: "The Academy has been guarded by Marines for the last two days, and all upperclass liberty outside the 7 mile limit has been cancelled for this weekend. Right now the domestic tranquility of the nation is really coming apart at the seams."

The midshipmen whose letters appear in this volume are from all over the United States. Many became career naval officers. One voluntarily resigned from the academy rather than face the humiliation of a forced dismissal for drunkenness. One left the academy, later to become a minister. Together, they represent a panorama of academy history. William McCann came to the Naval School in 1848, when the institution was barely three years old. Founded in 1845, the Naval School, as it was then called, had an odd mix of students. Grouped by the "date" of their warrants, the students were a combination of boys as young as thirteen and men as old as twenty-eight. The sea-experienced "oldsters" came to the Naval School for the academics they did not receive on board ship. The younger boys, or "youngsters," came to the school, passed an entrance examination, studied at the school for one year, and then went to sea for six months. Thereafter they earned a midshipman's warrant. Under such a system, William McCann did not graduate until 1854. In 1850 the Naval School became the Naval Academy and gradually moved toward a more traditional four-year program.

By the time Barry Mason Shambach began composing his Shambach Weekly Newsletter in 1967, the academy bore almost no resemblance to the original Naval School. However, Shambach's letters, the last in the collection, echo the concerns of earlier midshipmen. No matter the year of admission, no matter the decade or even the century, the letters share many concerns and problems, including acute homesickness, unreasonable upperclassmen, physical exhaustion, and the hope for a light at the end of the tunnel.

When I began reading these letters in November 1994, I was impressed by their immediacy and candor. As a parent whose own sons had left home, I found reassurance in the midshipmen's clear attachment to family and friends. As an academy professor who had developed a deep respect for the institution, I found the description of midshipman life enlightening. In 1995, when the academy celebrated its 150th anniversary, we turned to these letters as we created the birthday celebration for the sesquicentennial.

What emerges from these letters, then, is a unique history of the academy, written by young men who suffered all the anxieties and joys of their unique life. They write home asking for money or for a treasured item they had left behind. Eager for hometown news, many of the mids request a subscription to their local newspapers. In addition, the letters provide a unique glimpse of American history. Like their contemporary counterparts, these midshipmen were never far removed from national events. They grew accustomed to presidents in their midst, visiting dignitaries at parades, and the omnipresent possibility of being called to serve in armed conflict.

When I direct the Masqueraders here at the academy, I work for months with the students, creating a theatrical production. Day after day, weekend after weekend, the mids and I work on sets and costumes and blocking and lines. Nothing in the production moves forward without our joint efforts. However, when the show opens, I disappear, my efforts finished. I retire to the back of Mahan Hall, sitting behind the audience in a little window well, watching the students work their magic on stage—watching the audience appreciate the midshipmen in new ways.

My goal in editing these letters has been much the same—to step aside and allow each midshipman to emerge as a distinct personality. To that end, I have written introductions to each chapter, attempting to place the letters in the larger context of academy history. I have provided a glossary of useful terms, but I have chosen not to rely on footnotes to amplify the letters. Many mids refer to friends and family members who are strangers to us, yet the mention of such "strangers" indicates the young man's interest in people and places outside of his own small world. Thus, I have let such references stand. On a similar note, throughout this volume I have used the term "midshipmen" to refer to the students, although at times in academy history they were referred to by other titles.

The different writing styles reflect the times and the individuals. Some of the nineteenth-century correspondents, for example, write long paragraphs filled with very long sentences—long sentences that might seem in need of revision. I have done no such revising. Nor have I altered how dates are indicated on the letters. Some fellows cannot remember to include the date. Others use only numbers. Some pay attention to the date one week and ignore the calendar the next.

With the completion of this book, I once again retreat to the window well. These letter-writing mids, whom I have come to know and respect over the last few years, will now command center stage. What they have to say deserves an audience.

Letters from Annapolis

CHAPTER 1

The Prettiest Place in Maryland

The Letters of William Penn McCann

He had two strikes against him. At eighteen, he was too old, and the appointment he carried was in his brother's name, not his. Still, William McCann set out for the new Naval School from his Paris, Kentucky, home in 1848 determined to gain admission. He did. McCann successfully petitioned Secretary of the Navy John Mason on two counts. First, Mason waived the prohibition against admitting anyone over the age of seventeen. Second, the secretary ordered his chief clerk to write up new orders for McCann in his own name, not his brother's.

Secretary Mason's assessment of the young McCann's potential proved accurate. When McCann retired from the navy in 1892, he had reached the rank of commodore (rear admiral). From his first midshipman appointment on the frigate Raritan, McCann distinguished himself as an exceptional officer. His Civil War bravery, his South Pacific leadership, his administrative service combined to make him a credit to his family, to his hometown and to the Naval Academy. Known at his death in 1906 as the "Father of the White Squadron," McCann earned the nickname by suggesting that ships be painted white when they were in tropical countries, to deflect the intense heat.

But in 1848, the future Father of the White Squadron was an eighteen-year-old midshipman, with his Civil War bravery and South Pacific tours still ahead. He entered an institution that struggled with disciplinary and curricular issues, an institution still trying to discover the best way to train naval officers. McCann's letters capture his initial uncertainty about passing the required entrance examination and his ultimate pride in his success.

Writing home from the new Naval School, which had been founded in 1845,

William Penn McCann, later in his career *Courtesy USNA Nimitz Special Collections*

his exuberance is clear: "The Naval School is the prettiest place in Maryland"; "We have the best professors in the world"; "The boys here are the cream of America." As one of those boys, William McCann fulfilled the promise of the new institution.

OCTOBER 18 1848 ANNAPOLIS MARYLAND

Pa:

After one week's trouble I have reached my place of destination and reported to the Captain, who is Superintendent. The river being low caused me one day's delay in Marysville. I took passage in a sternwheel steamer to Pittsburgh, and then took a ticket to Baltimore, where I last night stopped. The reason I took that route was to save me one day and fifty miles staging. I paid the price to Pittsburgh on account of the river being low—went to Brownsville and Cumberland and then took the cars to this city where I arrived in one hour from Baltimore. I have just returned from the garrison (which is directly on the Chesapeake) with an arithmetic, which the Captain put in my hand to "rub up", as he called it, until next Monday when my examination takes place. I could have had it today, if I had wished but he suggested to me the plan I am pursuing. It will cost me five dollars till then when I shall have twenty left, not enough to come back with if I do not pass—but make yourself easy, as that is not my intention. At Pittsburgh I came across John Beattie, a son of a congressman from Butler County (back of Pittsburgh) on his way to this place on the same business with myself. Of course an immediate acquaintance sprung up. We are now together and will stay together. He is longer (not taller) than myself, though a good deal younger, and it is very possible that we will pass at the same time. We both have arithmetics, and are at a private boarding house, where we will stay till Monday—an awful day with me! By the way, in place of going to Washington, I saw Washington Monument in Baltimore, and that is enough of that. They will be very particular in the examination. The Captain even asked me how my time had been spent and how much money I had!—to which I gave prompt replies. At first he was as severe as an old devil, and in ten minutes, my friend. The school is under the severest rules and regulation of any place I have seen. It looks as clean as a parlor. Blue cloth and gold buttons and lace in plenty! I will have to pass a very severe examination. Ten days spent at home would have been worth much to me at this time. The next time I write I will do better than I am now doing and hope it will be a little more interesting. I had the finest kind of a trip—Much fun and fine provider!—though I came over the mountains in the night and missed a grand sight. I must discontinue. You shall hear from me as soon as I pass. I am now 830 miles from Paris, and such a thing is probable that by this time one year, I will be 8000! But this is the first "branching"—I paid 180 per day while in Baltimore—50 cents a meal on the road, and three prices on the boat—the reason I am now nearly out of money. If I had brought a trunk along it would have cost five dollars. I will write Monday. When you read this you will, in one respect, compare it to Clay's "I am" letter, but the similarity ceases there. Another letter five days from now.

Yours,

W. P. McCann

In looking over the morning papers I noticed that Secretary Mason has gone to Vermont to examine the docks, and my anticipated visit to Washington would have proven profitless.

All things for the best

W. P. M.

OCTOBER 21 1848 ANNAPOLIS MARYLAND

Brother John:

Since I first wrote I have had much difficulty and trouble, but I think it will soon be over. The day after I arrived I told the Captain of the appointment being in my brother's name. He then told me I must go to Washington and have it put in my name. After that I found my age would be a stumbling block, but I have just returned from a visit to the Captain and I think the sky is once more bright. I was by the Captain introduced to Professor Shuman, and we had a talk about the matter. They tell me if I can go see the Secretary and have a personal interview it will be alright. The Secretary is now away from the Capitol and Captain says

George Parker Upshur, superintendent 1847–50. "Captain Upshur has volunteered his best services in my behalf and if I get through I will owe it to his advice and instructions." *Courtesy USNA Nimitz Library Archives*

he will inform me of his return, when I shall hasten to Washington. The rule for admitting no person over seventeen is not a law, but is discretionary with the professors. Shuman tells me he will be easy with me and that my knowledge of perspective is worth a great deal to me, and will outweigh my age, and that will, I think, be no difficulty. In the meantime I will be as industrious as possible with my arithmetic and geography—the only two branches upon which I will be examined. There is a gentlemanly teacher at St. John's College, who has been helping me in my studies, and has volunteered to carry me through. He has taught others preparing them for examinations at the Naval School. I shall go to St. John's while the Secretary returns, and a week thereafter "pass" or do all that is possible. The Captain says if I pass it would be advisable for me to go to sea immediately. I am paying one dollar a day for board. The reason I am going to college is I can get my board and tuition for less than I am paying for board now. Captain Upshur has volunteered his best services in my behalf and if I get through I will owe it to his advice and instructions. There are seven at St. John's preparing themselves for examination—who did not pass and have had their time extended and will try it again. I heard their examination this morning and think I am better prepared than they will be at the end of two weeks. It will take a good deal of generalship to get in, but I think I will gain it after a few weeks good management. I will do my best—as long as my money lasts and there is any prospect of getting in—I shall not cease my exertions. Make yourself easy, if there is any prospect of getting in, I will succeed. George, I am confident, could not pass the physician's examination but Captain says he will underwrite for me! And that too with credit to myself and Old Kentuck. There is one lad in the college, intended for the Navy, who is over eighteen, who thinks he will have no difficulty; and another nearly as old as myself. None of them appreciates the position as I do, and certainly none will work as faithful as I will to obtain it. Tell Pa if Shackford has not paid for the canvas to take it home again, and to Larry Wilkins about my easel. Let none of my paintings be abused or misplaced. Give my regards to all,

Yours,
W. P. McCann

OCTOBER 27TH 1848 WASHINGTON D. C.

Brother John:

I have just returned from the Secretary's office. You cannot imagine what a straight I have gone through. So far all is well. (Excuse bad writing for I am in such a glee I can scarcely write at all). I thought once or twice that I will have to return home, but I shall not do that. The Secretary asked me how old I was, to which I promptly replied. He read to me the regulations (not laws) about those matters; he said it was against their regulation to admit any into the service over seventeen—called up a Chief Clerk, and told him to give me orders in my name, which he did—and which I have in my possession. When I was taking leave of Mason I could say no more than "Good Morning"—but he understood my feelings, and I was satisfied.

My appointment is to report tomorrow or as shortly thereafter as possible. I shall wait and study another week—then, one more trial, and I will be through! I will hasten to Annapolis in the evening train (I came up yesterday evening) and study hard. The examination is a small affair. I have been all through the Capitol—saw the painting in the Rotunda and that vacant panel which, if I was able, I would rather fill with a design of my own. . . . I shall visit the National Institute and the Navy Yard before I leave, if I can. I came up from the junction of the Railroad with Mr. Upshur, a clerk in the Navy Department—a nephew of the Captain and the Secretary who was killed on board the Princeton, down in the Potomac River. The nine days I was at Annapolis I studied part at St. John's and some at my boarding house. I was in the Senate chamber and saw Sully's picture of Carrolton and Judge somebody!—and I stood on the spot where Washington resigned his commission to the Continental Congress, in the Old State House of Maryland, built before the Revolution. I have now about twelve dollars in my purse, but I can get a complete set of uniforms with far less than my travelling expenses which will be ten cents per mile—83 dollars in all. I intended visiting the President, but I shall not stay until tonight—this is his evening to receive visitors. At 4 o clock I shall start back to Annapolis. You must direct your letters there. I have been in some anxiety for about a week, but I have taken everything easy. Write to me soon. I am now stopping at the Willard House. I stopped at the Eutaw House in Baltimore. I always stop at the best houses wherever I go. This letter is about me, myself—very full of "I"—hope the next will be more interesting.

Your brother,
W. P. McCann

BRIGHT WEDNESDAY NOVEMBER 1 1848
ANNAPOLIS MARYLAND

Pa:

I have just stood my "examination"; it was as it always is a hard place, but I came off with flying colors—the result of my application. It is twenty days since I started from home on this trip, and I am now successful and thankful for it. I have left now seven or eight dollars. I shall give my friend, Mr. Thompson, five of them; and will have about what will pay my board since my return from Washington, and then "be out." There are seven or eight with appointments at St. John's College. They will have to work hard before they get through. There is no partiality shown. Most of the appointees are Congressmen's sons, or, if not, favorites of those in power, but the professors are the finest set of men I have seen or known, and with them, there is no partiality—not its shadow. At one time during my examination the perspiration started from every pore—'twas on a sum in denomination, but I got through that straight and I expect I shall get through some more straights before long—but I think it will be the straights of Gibraltar or some other of that kind. When Lieutenant Lee informed me of the decision of the Academic Board, he said he was happy "to inform me that I was found duly qualified to be one of the U.S. N." I made a very graceful bow and replied that I was happy to hear it; then he told me to sleep contented tonight, and call up in the morning, after breakfast, which, of course, I shall do. The course of studies in the school is a thorough course of Mathematics and Navigation, and almost everything (French included) except Theology. The older Naval officers and "middies" stand at the "top" in every part of the world. About Christmas, the students will have fourteen days to go where they please. I wish I had my pictures of "Napoleon" here—I could cut quite a dash among everybody. Write to me soon, and tell all to write—give my love and regards to everybody at grandpa's and home. Write everything that would be interesting and write immediately. Polk will visit the school tomorrow, and I shall go to see him. After all he founded the institution, and of course we will salute him very elegantly when he arrives. Yesterday Governor Thomas was visited by the Sharp Shooters of Baltimore, to whom he gave a splendid dinner. He and everybody else here is democratic—that is all those in office. The State is Whig and will go largely for Taylor—as you will see in a few days. Tell John I thought of the telegraph whilst in Washington but thought it useless to attempt a communication by it. I must close.

Yours,
W. P. McCann

See how this looks "W. P. McCann, U. S. N. !"

NOVEMBER 6, 1848 NAVAL SCHOOL ANNAPOLIS MARYLAND

Pa:

I have just received your letter by which I find you had not received a letter I wrote you from Washington, informing you of my success. I passed my examination on the first of November. Remember this as it may be a matter of importance in the future. I am now on the list as an applicant for sailing orders, which I am assured by the Captain I shall receive. He is a brother of the Secretary who was killed on board the Princeton a few years since. He is an old and experience Naval Officer and is like a father to all the officers. Being an officer I will have to buy a "cocked hat" and sword and a quadrant for telling latitudes and longitudes and time of day, a Boroditch, and several suits of clothes—socks, shirts, and those things by the dozen—when I leave in the "Raritan." I am confident I will receive my orders in a few days as the Captain is compelled to detail officers to fit out that vessel—which is a frigate—the most pleasant vessel in the world to go to sea in. It will go to the Gulf and then to the Mediterranean sea—on a cruise of three years. It is the policy of the Secretary and all the officers in the Navy to keep the Midshipmen here as long as possible, before going to sea. I have now the choice of staying here or going to sea—the latter I have selected. My studies are Composition, Grammar, French, Arithmetic—but the full course is a thorough course of Mathematics, Navigation, etc. You cannot think of a science that is not taught here. Steamworks and Gunnery are

The Naval School, 1848. "The Naval School is the prettiest place in Maryland. . . . The buildings are principally yellow brick with green blinds." *Courtesy USNA Nimitz Library Archives*

the most important. The boys here are the cream of America:—fifteen "youngsters" and fifty "Oldsters," Officers, professors, etc. We all live together like brothers. We have plenty of oysters for dinner—a splendid table for which there is a deduction from our wages of $19 per month. We are allowed $30 per month whilst here and $40 and rations whilst at sea. It will take $200 to fit one out for sea—two or three months pay in advance would be sufficient. I came 830 miles and will receive $83 for my travelling expenses—Very probably I will receive this day after tomorrow, out of which I will pay twenty dollars, I am owing. I will have what will take me to my vessel and something considerably over, to help me to outfit. The Naval School is the prettiest place in Maryland, directly on the Chesapeake Bay, and on the Severn River which empties in at this place. This was once Fort Severn—a very important place once. The buildings are principally yellow brick with green blinds. The Recitation Halls are beautiful rooms, with carpets and desks like the Senate Chamber at Washington and in the State House here. We have the best professors in the world. Our rooms are clean and neatly furnished—Iron bedsteads and green bedding! I have just bought half a dozen shirts, towels, pillowcases, etc. and can get credit for 500 dollars should I wish it. I have countermanded an order for a coat, jacket, vest, two pair pants, which I had ordered of the finest deep-blue cloth, trimmed with buttons of gold, with anchors of the same material on the shoulders. The gold band around my cap tells where I am. Imagine how one of my size will look in a cocked hat, commanding on board the "Raritan." The reason I will not get my clothes here is the Captain says I had better get them at the place I start from and suitable to the climate where I shall go. When you write to me direct to "Midshipman," and it will come directly to the school. I will write before I go to sea. Write soon, and tell me all that would be interesting.

I remain,
W. P. McCann

P.S. When the above was written I was not sworn in. I have just taken the oath and am now an "Acting Midshipman." There are about twenty papers and articles to sign. Within is my letter of acceptance which I wrote to the Secretary. There is a good library here, especially for the use of naval scholars. Tomorrow I receive my expenses. Tell John and George to write. I am anxious to hear from them. Tell me all about Paris!

Your Son
W. P. McCann

CHAPTER 2

Those Demerits Are a Perfect Humbug

The Letters of Josiah G. Beckwith Jr.

"The thing of dismissing a man from a great national institution like this for so trivial a thing as getting two hundred demerits is outrageous." As Josiah Beckwith wrote these words, he was referring to one of his classmates facing imminent dismissal. He did not know that shortly, his would be a similar fate. In the early years of the Naval Academy, the student body was a mix of inexperienced new appointees as young as thirteen and experienced sailors who might be in their late twenties. The son of a prominent physician and state legislator, Beckwith was fifteen years old when he entered the academy in 1853. Unfortunately, his stay at Annapolis was troubled and short.

Although Beckwith liked the academy, he complained that "the discipline is very severe." That severity forced Beckwith to resign in 1855, when he was "persuaded to drink" by a group of friends. Even before the drinking incident, his conduct records indicate many demerits given for minor offenses. His correspondence captures the young man's frustrating attempts to reduce his number of demerits.

Trying to prevent his son's 1855 dismissal, Dr. Beckwith wrote to Superintendent Louis M. Goldsborough, who had a reputation for leniency, that Josiah "had not been exposed to the bad influences of society" and thus was "not proof against the corrupting influences of large assemblies of young men." Given the mix of ages at the Naval School, there is some validity to the concerned father's reasoning. Even though his reputation for leniency seriously diminished his leadership ability, Goldsborough did not tolerate drunkenness. The young Beckwith was given a choice: resignation or dismissal. Vowing never to touch another "drop of liquor," Josiah Beckwith chose to resign.

ANNAPOLIS MARCH 5 1853

Dear Father,

Your very welcome letter of the 28th came to hand on the 2nd and also one of the 22nd containing the key to my trunk. I applied to Captain Stribling for leave to go to Washington for twenty four hours, but there were so many applications at the same time that he was obliged to refuse me. I wrote the same afternoon to Mr. Seymour to apply to the Secretary for two or three days leave. (It is not likely I shall take more than one to come down to Washington and see him about my getting a furlough as I thought I should be able to explain the case more fully to him than you could from my letter.) But if I get leave from the Secretary I cannot draw any money to pay my expenses, so if you could conveniently enclose five or six dollars in a letter and direct it to J.G.B. and charge the same to my account you will oblige me very much. I came off the list Friday not so much because I was any better as to get rid of the Doctor's drugs. Surgeons in the Navy employ the very harshest and most disagreeable medicine, probably to prevent persons from coming on the list unless they are very sick. If that is their object I think they have succeeded wonderfully, for I think that I should prefer to go sick sometime before I would go on the list again. My roommate Mr. Ashe recovered some time ago. He has gone now to Washington on five days leave. Our friends, Bishop and Sutherland, of whom you speak in one of your letters, have returned to their anxious friends in company with several other young men. On an average not more than one third of every date pass through the Institution so that it takes a pretty smart scholar to pass. Professor Chauvenet (first professor in Mathematics) said at the recitation this morning that we had to pass a very thorough examination next time in Geography, Grammar and Arithmetic besides those studies which we pursue this summer, and if we don't pass the examination we are to be sent home. So I think my chance is rather slim if I stay here. The weather is very variable. Day before yesterday it rained very hard. Yesterday it was very beautiful and today it commenced snowing about noon and has continued ever since. I suppose you are having fine sleighing in Litchfield now. Do Elizabeth and the children take many sleigh rides? How long is it since Mother has been out to Milton? I wish I was there to eat some of Mrs. Welch's nice dinner. Yesterday I sent out and got a dozen of eggs. Last night I boiled half of them in my tin bucket after the drum had beat for lights to be out. It is not necessary to say whether I ate them or not. Captain Stribling is going to leave next June as no officer in the Navy can remain in one place more than six years and he should have last summer been gone by rights. I hope we shall get as good a man to take his place. We are to have a brass band instead of the drum and fife next summer and also a dancing master which I think will be a decided acquisition to us. I have not yet received my trunk but have no doubt it is at the depot. I shall go out this afternoon and see about it. You speak in your letter of taking the cake in homeopathic doses. I think that doctrine applies better to some kinds of drugs than to eatables, cake in particular. A change is talked of in the uniform of Acting Mids by substituting the Frock coat for the jacket. I think as far as I am concerned the change would be very agreeable. I have been having my blue frock coat changed to an undress military by having brass Navy buttons put on. The legislature is still in session here. We have no news of importance. Do you keep Sam yet? I expect to have a good many rides after him if I come home this summer. We had a queer occurrence in the Battery this morning. Mr. Latimer (the professor in gunnery) pointed a gun at the target (which is ¾ of a mile off). The ball went straight till it neared the target when it made a curve and went nearly around it. It was probably owing to the floor giving when the gun went off. It is now near supper time and I must close my letter. Give my love to mother and the children, not forgetting Uncle George and thanks very much for taking The Republican for me, which I read with more interest than I ever did before. I wish you would send me the Journal of Commerce once and awhile if you still take it, as we do not get the news here till about a month after the rest of the world. Give my love to all inquiring friends and tell Benedict to write to me.

Yours affectionately,
J. G. Beckwith

NAVAL ACADEMY MARCH 1853

Dear Father,

Your letter of the 20th was duly received. I was not aware that so long a time had elapsed since I had written to you till I chanced to come across your letter in my drawer. I received a letter the other day dated February 1. It had two postmarks: one Litchfield and the other Memphis, Tennessee, from which I concluded that our letter had taken a rather roundabout way of reaching here. The watch was received in good order; it did not seem to have suffered from its journey with the exception of its face being slightly loosened. I have sent it out to be fixed. It will not cost but a trifle and will be none the worse for travel. I think that it is a very beautiful watch. It is substantial and at the same time looks neat and tasteful. I shall not return my thanks for it now. I shall wait till I come home next summer. . . . I think that you have a very mistaken idea in regard to demerits: it is not the faculty who give demerits but an executive officer and his assistant. The executive officer is Captain Craven and his assistant is Lieutenant Marcy for whose honesty I cannot say much. Demerits are not given for serious offenses (for such you are suspended or reported to the secretary) but for little trifling omissions, such as being late or absent from roll call when perhaps you did not hear the drum beat; or for stepping into a neighboring room for a book to find out how a lesson is in study hours. This comes under the head of visiting during study hours and is two demerits. I will send you a copy of the regulations. The most reasonable regulations are printed in this, but those that they would prefer not to be seen come under the head of "internal regulations;" but enough of this. I have been on the list for hoarseness since Thursday but am now much better. You asked me in your last letter in regard to my length, weight, size, and so forth. As near as I can remember it is as follows. Height: 6 feet 1½ inches; Weight, 163 lbs.; Measurement: 36 inches around the chest. I sent you a naval register the other day which you have doubtless received before this. I receive The Republican regularly. I suppose that old Litchfield is very dull about these times. Nevertheless, I would like very much to be there, dull as it is. Give my love to all the family.

Your affectionate son,

J. G. Beckwith

ANNAPOLIS APRIL 4 1853

Dear Father,

Your good long letter of the 1st was received this afternoon and also a prescription for my throat which I shall have put up at my first opportunity. My throat is getting better every day, but still I think it would be best to have it cured up at once. There is no regulation that I have ever heard against a midshipman getting or using any medication which he chooses. I also found enclosed a gold piece for which I thank you very much. I have just been getting me made a pea coat or midshipman's over coat. I think that I shall find it very useful next summer on board the Preble, expecially on night watches and stormy days. It has been raining very hard all day and part of last night but this evening it is clearing off. I like my new roommate Mr. Cameron very much. He is very quiet and gentlemanly and I think will make a good student. He is a nephew of General Cameron, U.S. Senator. My new room is situated on the first floor and is a much pleasanter room than the one which I have just left. The building is the last of the row and nearest the battery. The walls and floor are a little defaced as the room has lately been occupied by some pretty hard cases, but I have been promised that it will be fixed up before long, and then my roommate and myself intend to have it fitted up in style with carpet, curtains and a new table cover, new lamp, etc. We have a grate instead of a stove in our room which I think is much more cheerful. This week I drew from the library the Koran or the Mohammedan Bible. It is very powerfully written and I am very much interested in it. We are having several buildings erected which employ a great many laborers, but there's no news of importance in the yard. There is a report about that Captain Craven, Commander of Midshipmen, has been ordered away, but how true the report is I could not say. Last week, Captain Stribling reported three acting midshipmen to the Secretary for having more than two hundred demerits. They will probably be pronounced deficient in conduct and dismissed from the Navy. There are now seven or eight who are on the verge of two hundred and will have to go soon. Mr. Sutherland has written home for permission to resign on account of his having nearly two hundred demerits. Our date is getting a good many demerits, mostly on drill. There is scarcely one in our date who has less than fifty, but these will not count on us on account of our being new beginners and besides the demerits of everyone in the Academy are taken off next June and ours with the rest. I have not heard positively whether I go to England or not, but should judge from what I hear that it is very likely I shall go. It is now nearly bed time and I must close my letter. Good night. Give my love to all.

Your affectionate son,
J. G. Beckwith

ANNAPOLIS APRIL 1853

Dear Mother,

It is long since I promised to write you, but my time has been so much occupied with my studies, exercise, etc that I have not had the leisure to do so till the present time. Today is Saturday, but as it is not my time to go out, this afternoon I have nothing to do but to write letters. It is now nearly three months since I left you one cold January morning to start for the Naval School. Since that time I have seen considerable of the world and have found a good many queer people in it, and also found to my perfect satisfaction that there is no place like home. I am very much pleased with the Naval Academy notwithstanding that the discipline is very severe. My time is so completely filled up that I cannot find any time to idle if I was so disposed. We have so much time allowed to us for our meals, so much for study hours and just so long a time to get each lesson in, so much for recreation, and so much for sleep. By the way, I must tell you what kind of bed I have to sleep on. We have a little iron bedstead, a little more than six feet long and just wide enough to balance yourself in without tumbling out. On this we have a mattress and a pillow, each as hard as a board, two blankets, one sheet. This is our equipment in the sleeping line. Our buildings are all made of brick. The rooms are large, well lighted and warmed. Beside this we have three hundred dollars a year allowed us by the government, which is enough to support us handsomely. Our board is acceptable, though of course not quite as good as you are used to at home, but on the whole, we are very

The Lyceum, mess hall and recitation hall. "At half past six every morning every mid and acting mid in the yard meet for prayer at the Lyceum." *Courtesy USNA Nimitz Library Archives*

comfortably situated. Every afternoon, Saturday and Sunday excepted, we drill from four to half past five. At six we have dress parade. Every one is required to come out in full uniform, white gloves, etc. If your gloves are a little soiled or shoes not well blacked, you are reported and get four demerits. After parade, we march in to supper. At half past six every morning every mid and acting mid in the yard meet for prayer at the Lyceum. After prayer, we have what is called undress parade. We are not required to be in full uniform and have no muskets. At dinner we have the same. So you see that on the whole, we are kept pretty busy, but enough of this. I find that our date or rather our portion of it are to go to Sea for three years in succession and allowing four months to a cruise will make an entire year of sea service in the four years which we stay here, being 4 months more than it is usual for a date to have. So by the time we get through we shall be pretty good seamen, which will give us a great advantage over the others. It is now just six weeks before I can get a furlough to come home. I anticipate a great deal of pleasure from seeing all my friends again, although my stay will be a short one. How is your health now? Are your eyes still as painful to you as when I left? If they are, when you answer this, you must not write after your eyes commence paining you. Love to all,

Your affectionate son,
J. G. Beckwith

ANNAPOLIS APRIL 1853

Dear Father,

Your very welcome letter of the 11th was duly received yesterday afternoon. I should have answered it yesterday but my time was so much occupied with studies, drills, etc that I had no time to do so. We have just had a fine shower which lasted nearly an hour and passing off left everything much fresher. I am glad to hear that Edward B. is coming to spend the summer with you. I should think he would make a very good clerk in the store as well as company for you this summer. When does Benedict think of attending lectures? I am glad to hear that you are going to build a new barn. I think it will be a decided improvement. Last Monday night we had quite an excitement in Annapolis. An old Ten Pin Alley caught on fire or was set on fire and entirely burned down. We were started out at about eight o clock by the drum beating to quarters. Our engine, the Severn, was brought out manned but before it reached the fire it was nearly out. So we amused ourselves with throwing water on the crowd and adjoining houses and came home at about eleven after having a pretty good time of it. . . . About my demerits, I have not got a single report against me this week, so far, and I intend to try and not get any more if I can possibly help it. I have been a little negligent in regard to some of my recitations since I have been here. I have never made any bad ones, but there are some which I could have made better if I had studied a little harder. This was owing in a great degree to my room mate whose habits were very loose. This morning I made a resolution that hereafter I would always fully prepare all my lessons before going into recitation. In this way I can shortly get a reputation of being a good scholar which will stay by me while I stay at the Academy. I know that you feel anxious in regard to me and are somewhat fearful as to how I will eventually turn out. But I hope that I may never do any thing which may cause you pain or to regret the confidence which you have placed in me. . . .

Your affectionate son,

J. G. Beckwith

U.S. NAVAL ACADEMY NOVEMBER 8 1853

Dear Father,

Your letters of the 31st and 8th were duly received. I am sorry to hear that Uncle George is sick but hope that he will be nearly well by the time that you will receive this. We had quite a serious accident happen in the Yard the other day. Midshipman Totten (son of General Totten of the Army) it seems was sitting in a second story window but by some means lost his balance and fell out striking his side on the pavement and his head on the corner of the doorstep, cutting his head terribly. He was soon after found by some one who was passing that way and taken to his room. During the night the Surgeon gave him up but I believe that he is now nearly out of danger. Captain Goldsborough the present Superintendent is a perfect tyrant. I hope that I shall never have the bad luck to have anything to do with him. About that clock please exercise your own taste in the matter and whatever suits you will suit me. Never mind the pants this time. I will send you a sample of the cloth and you can get them made at your leisure. Do you know who the officer was that Uncle George met in New York? I have not seen or heard anything of him. I received a letter from Elizabeth yesterday. All's well in P. It is so near dinner time that I must close. Love to all.

Your affectionate son,

J. G. Beckwith

JANUARY 15TH 1854

Dear Father,

Your letter of the 30th was duly received. It should have been answered some time ago. This is the second or third week that I have al-

Louis Goldsborough, superintendent 1853–57. "Captain Goldsborough the present superintendent is a perfect tyrant." *Courtesy USNA Nimitz Library Archives*

lowed to pass without writing. I will endeavor not to have this occur again. I have been expecting Mr. Seymour down here for several weeks but I suppose that he is so busy in Washington that he has not the time to spare. I should very much like to see Uncle John and his wife in Annapolis this winter. I think they would find the climate much pleasanter this time of the year than farther north. The clock arrived here on New Year's Day and I assure you was a very acceptable New Year's present.

The clock is a very pretty one and is much admired. What is the price of such a clock at retail? I have been asked the price. Christmas and New Years passed off very pleasantly with us. On the Monday after Christmas all the acting midshipmen had permission to draw from the purser one dollar for every ten that we had there deposited. And to visit Annapolis and the vicinity during the day. Do you intend coming down here to see me this winter? You will find the Academy very much changed. So much so that you would hardly recognize it as the same place. The Secretary says that those of the 53 date that went to sea last year will have a three months leave next summer while the others go to sea. This is very good news to me for I shall have leave to go home two summers running. This next summer while the rest of my class are at sea and the summer after that when I go home with the rest of my date. You have undoubtedly received my monthly standing before this. I am aware that it is not a very encouraging one but I think that I shall be able to send you a much more favorable one next month. I went into demerits pretty extensively last month but I could not help it. 15 of my demerits were for things I did not do and many others were unavoidable. However demerits have but a multiple of 5 this year and most of my date have as many or more than I. Our February examination is very simple and I am prepared to stand it, so you need not give yourself any uneasiness on that score. You may rest assured that I will not disgrace either myself or my friends by being dismissed from the service. I think that you must have rather a small family at home now, only you, Mother and the two children. I think that you can safely calculate for one more next summer. I should very much like to see old Litchfield and all the kind friends again. Where is Benedict now? If you have his address please send it to me. The weather is cool, though by no means cold here. Give my love to mother and all the family.

Your affectionate son,
J. G. Beckwith

U.S. NAVAL ACADEMY JANUARY 1854

Dear Father,

Your letter of the 16th was duly received. You have probably received mine of last week. You speak of my having so many demerits. I acknowledge that I have got a good many, many more than perhaps I should have, but there were twelve or fifteen more put down than by good rights belonged to me. I shall endeavor to get some or all of them taken off. Ours has been a great date for getting demerits. There are but a few that have less than I have and a great many who have over a hundred and a hundred and fifty. There are four or five who have over two hundred which you know is their compliment this month. I have but 4 so far. I think that I shall be able to stand a very good examination. I intend making a general review of all the studies before the examination. I received the 2.50 gold piece and thought that I had mentioned it before. I should have done so. Mr. Seymour and Edward were down here last week. Mr. Seymour came in the evening time and went away at six in the morning. Edward stayed over the next day. Mr. Cook was with him. I should very much like to see you and mother down here after the examination. I doubt your being able to get me leave to meet you in New York. It is now a little over a year since you left me here. And you can imagine how I should like to see you and mother again after a year's separation. The weather is very cold today. It has been one of the coldest days we have had this season. There is no news of any importance in Annapolis. Give my love to Mother and all the family not forgetting Uncle John and Aunt Rachel.

Your affectionate son,
J. G. Beckwith

U.S. NAVAL ACADEMY APRIL 12 1854

Dear Father,

Your letter of the 10th was duly received this afternoon. In relation to my having 20 demerits last month, it is entirely a mistake. I had 18 before I saw Captain G.—but none afterwards; he sends home 5 demerits less on my report than are put up on the board for our inspection. So instead of having 192 demerits, I have but 187 leaving out the 30 that Captain G—took off. I intended to go down and have the mistake in my report rectified and also see why the 30 which the Captain took off have not been deducted. I was very sorry to learn through Elizabeth that Uncle John's splint factory has been burned. Did it prove a total loss? I came down several numbers last month on account of my sickness—not indeed within the reach of danger but a little lower than I like to stand but I shall probably come up again next month. . . . The Secretary said that those who went to sea last summer would have a furlough this summer: but he may make some different arrangements before June—so do not calculate on my coming home as a certainty, as there is a chance of my being disappointed: however, I hope this will not happen. For should I not come home this summer, it will be nearly two years and a half before I come home which is a long time to go without seeing one's friends. But "it is an ill wind that blows nobody any good" and if I do not come home till summer after next, I shall have $200 to come home with; while if I come home this summer I shall not have but $75 or $80. You asked me in one of your previous letters "whether Bishop resigned or was dismissed the first time." He was dismissed and was afterward reinstated. It appears to me that if I was driven to such an extremity that I should much prefer to resign; for a resignation is considered perfectly honorable and attaches no stigma to the name—while on the other hand a dismissal is considered a disgrace, and it will always adhere to a man, let his afterlife be what it will.

The weather is very changeable. In one day the temperature will be delightful and the next we will have high winds. This climate is remarkable for its changeableness during the spring. I wish that you would send me some sasparilla syrup. My blood, I think, is rather impure. Please send it by express and also directions on how to use it. Hoping that this will find all the family in good health.

I remain your affectionate son,

J. G. Beckwith

Samuel L. Marcy, one of the original faculty members at the Naval School. "That Marcy is as mean a scoundrel as was ever permitted to live." *Courtesy USNA Nimitz Library Archives*

U.S. NAVAL ACADEMY NOVEMBER 24, 1854

Dear Father,

I have not any news to communicate today yet as I have leisure, I will employ it in writing to you. I suppose that demerits are your chief source of anxiety now. Well, I have not got any so far: and if I can say so a week from this time, I shall have completed the month without any.

That Marcy is as mean a scoundrel as was ever permitted to live. He is a smart man, for a man has got to be smart to be a regular built rascal.

I am leader of a drawing section of about forty. Day before yesterday when we marched up to the recitation hall Marcy reported me for being disorderly in ranks. . . . Now this report was clearly false and made upon suspicion, for I was section leader and therefore not in ranks at all. And as for being disorderly, I had plenty to attend to to keep a section of forty in order without skylarking myself. The excuse that I wrote will take off the demerits which would accrue from the offences. There is no change in anything at the Academy. A dancing master is to be allowed to the Second and Third classes, so that each class will have dancing lessons given for two years. Our weather now is exceeding fine. It appears like Indian summer. Perhaps it is. Tell Mother that I am not particular as to the pattern that my shirts are made by. If they only fit that is all that is required. . . . Your letter of the 21st has been brought in this moment while I am writing. . . . I am sorry that Mother is not well. She must not in any way trouble or worry herself about those shirts. I can have them made here just as well. I am much pleased to hear of Sarah's rapid improvements. Tell her that she must write to me and tell me all about everything she is doing. I think that it is an advantage to a person to learn early how to express their ideas in a clear, tangible manner. I have always found it a good rule in letter writing to express my ideas as nearly as possible as if I were in actual conversation with the person to whom I am writing. Although of course I would be more careful of the language that I used and composition. However, I do not suppose that those rules of mine will be of any interest to you, so we will close this subject. I received the $ enclosed in your letter for which I am much obliged. It is now so near dinner time that I cannot write any more.

Your affectionate son,
J. G. Beckwith

US NAVAL ACADEMY MAY 20TH 1854

Dear Father,

Your letters of the 15th were duly received. How many demerits came home on my report for last month? Are not the thirty removed? I stopped in at the executive officer's office the other day and asked him in relation to them. He told me that Captain Goldsborough had ordered thirty to be removed and that they would be taken off before my report went home. I had previously desired him to see Captain G and ascertain what he intended to do in the matter. You asked me to tell you what I got my demerits for last month. One report was for firing on drill before the word: my excuse was that the Captain of the company next to ours gave the command fire, just at the time that ours should have done so and I, in common with over half of the company, thought that the command came from our Captain and fired accordingly. Another was for being last at section formation: my excuse to this was that I was in my room but the wind was so high that I could not hear the bugle. With the exception of two of three, they were all for things that I could not possibly by any prudence or foresight have avoided. I now have not had a single demerit for more than three weeks. I did not get any demerits for three weeks after I saw Captain G. I think that you have a mistaken idea of the arrangement that I made with Captain G. to have the thirty demerits taken off. The Captain did not take them off immediately on my application, but said that he would remove some if I would go without getting any for a spell and he saw that I was trying my best not to get any. About a fortnight after that I had this conversation with him, he called me down to his office and asked me if I had got any demerits since he had seen me. On my replying in the negative, he removed thirty of my demerits for which kindness I shall always feel grateful. Captain Goldsborough is a very clever man and has many good points, but he has his weak points of character, as has everyone else. Among other things, he has rather an undue opinion of his own importance. Now it is a very good thing to have a good opinion of yourself, but there is such a thing as having too much of a good thing, and it is bad to have a better opinion of yourself than other people have of you. And while talking to him he seems to make an effort to impress you with a sense of his dignity and importance, which makes it very disagreeable to hold a conversation with him. I remember a rather laughable story that is told of him. He has a son about sixteen years old. Though the boy is well enough, the father tries to make too much of him. One day he was extolling him to some gentleman and among other things mentioned that he did not seem like a boy. He talked like an old man of forty. Young Goldsborough who was standing near, but did not hear the remark, just at that moment turned around and hallowed out to another boy, "Bigelow, let's play tag." The effect can be imagined. But enough of this. I do not apprehend any danger from demerits. I have less than 170 and I am confident that I can avoid getting any between this and June. . . . I see that my paper is nearly exhausted and I must close my letter. Give my love to mother, the children, and all the rest of the family.

Your affectionate son,
J. G. Beckwith

ANNAPOLIS JANUARY 23 1855
Dear Father,

I received your letter of the 15th and 19th. You said in your last that you had enclosed a dollar; but on examining the letter, my disappointment was great on not finding one. Did you neglect to enclose it or has the letter been opened?

In relation to the study gown, I will get my measure taken for it next Saturday and send it on.

I have received a short letter from Elizabeth since her arrival in New Haven, stating her address, etc.

Sutherland who had so long meditated resigning, did so, a day or so ago. His acceptance is expected in a short time. Sutherland was a fine young fellow with talents of the highest order. He would have passed through without any difficulty, although he did not study any of consequence, if he had chosen.

You need not fear of my wishing to resign. I like the place too much to do anything of that kind. I have made up my mind to stay here, and I have strong doubts as to whether they would ever be able even to kick me out. The life on a regular man of war is very different from that on a practice ship, and I think that after giving the service a fair trial, I shall like it. At least, I shall give it a trial. . . . I am afraid that poor Colt will go again. He has got about one hundred and ninety demerits. He stands well enough in his studies, but his demerits will dismiss him. Those demerits are a perfect humbug. They are mostly given for trivial things, inadvertences and often for occurrences which you could not prevent. All the offences for which they are given are not put down in the regulations. They have what are called internal regulations: made up of orders and one thing or another, given by the different Superintendents who have been here. And the thing of dismissing a man from a great national institution like this for so trivial a thing as getting two hundred demerits, is outrageous. They are necessary for preserving discipline in the institution, but I think that the penalty is too severe. However, I intend to avoid them as far as possible. . . . My paper warns me that it is time to close. Love to all.

Yours affectionately,
J. G. Beckwith

U.S. NAVAL ACADEMY FEBRUARY 27, 1855

Dear Uncle,

It has become my painful task to inform my friends of an act that I have been guilty of, and which will be a source of the deepest regret to me as long as I live.

On last Saturday night I allowed myself to be persuaded to drink with some of my friends: it was the first, and I have taken an oath that it shall be the last time. I was unused to the effects of liquor, and a quantity that did not materially affect them, affected me in a much greater degree. I was discovered and the next morning was reported to Captain Goldsborough. Several others were reported at the same time.

Captain G. threatened to report us to the Secretary: I immediately wrote to Seymour and stated the case exactly as it stood, and requested him, if the case was reported to the Secretary, to use all his influence on my behalf.

I do not see how this can result in dismissal, for half a dozen cases have occurred in the Academy during the last two months, none of whom resulted in a serious manner. Many of these were not reported to the Secretary.

I write you this, because I think that it is possible that Capt G. will write to Father, and it will be much better for them to hear the facts from me than from an official paper. Do not show this to Father if this is not the case for I am anxious to spare him from this information.

I hope that I shall hear the decision on this soon: for I am very nervous on the subject.

My friends need not fear a repetition of this by me: not another drop of liquor will I drink.

I have not time to write anymore. Please let me hear from you immediately.

Your affectionate nephew,
J. G. Beckwith

CHAPTER 3

Civil War Is a Terrible Thing

The Letters of Oliver Ambrose Batcheller

By the time Oliver Ambrose Batcheller arrived at the U.S. Naval Academy in 1859, the already crowded academy was quickly running out of dormitory space for the increased student body. The administration, desperate for room, transformed the sloop Plymouth *into a school ship for the incoming class. Batcheller vividly described life aboard that ship. Lashing the hammock he slept in became a great challenge for the young New Yorker, but the greater challenge came as the Civil War simmered and then erupted. The specter of fighting against his fellow classmates haunted Batcheller, as the fate of the academy became increasingly unclear. Rumors flew: Maryland has seceded; a mob will attack the USNA; the academy will close. Finally, in late April 1861, the students left Annapolis on the school ship* Constitution *and sailed north. For the next four years, Newport, Rhode Island, became the academy's home.*

In 1861 Batcheller and his classmates were ordered into active duty. As the war broke out Batcheller enthusiastically responded to the effort: "The North has responded to the call for volunteers and I hope that the same spirit will continue to prevail until every insult which our flag and government have received shall be wiped out with blood." A career naval officer, Batcheller retired in 1891 as a commander. He died in 1893.

USS PLYMOUTH   NOVEMBER 30, 1859

Dear Father and Mother,

I now improve this opportunity of writing you a line with further information. You would be pleased to look in here and see your "son" as he appears on board ship. Let me give you the picture. 100 young fellows

Oliver Ambrose Batcheller *Courtesy USNA Nimitz Special Collections*

shut up in this little tub all full of fun (subscriber excepted) and argus eyed. Officers on every side and if you don't step just so "straighten up" greets your ear and I guess you straighten up some. The sleeping machine is this: a piece of canvas, 6 by 2½ feet, slung up by the ends and yourself comfortably laid in there and you will have something of an idea. I like the way of sleeping very well.

As for eating, I can find no faults with the food for there is enough of it and that pretty good. A nigger waiter to each table.

By the way I must tell you that the one who has the longest arm fares the best. . . . We have 14 at our mess and the motto is "God helps those who help themselves."

Upon the whole I like it very well here and think I can accquit myself with credit. The opportunities for education are unsurpassed and it is only on this account that I am particularly "taken up" with my recitation.

We have to go through with all the maneuvering of the ship: reefing sails, managing great guns and practicing small arms is part of our daily exercises. I don't have anything more to write except that if I behave myself very well I expect to go to Washington about Christmas on three days leave and six dollars pay. We are allowed seven dollars per month spending money. Our board costs 2 dollars per month. The rest goes to pay for clothes and the balance is paid when we graduate (if ever).

Give my love to all.

Yours as ever,
O. A. Batcheller
Acting Midshipman, USNA

USS PLYMOUTH DECEMBER 5, 1859

Dear Brother,

Having a few leisure moments, I thought I would give you a more detailed account of matters and things. I wrote you before under very peculiar circumstances and cannot now remember a word except that I told you I thought I should go to Washington at Christmas. . . . I am not certain now whether I shall go or not but whether I do or not it makes no difference. When I wrote that letter I was so confused by the noise and novelty of things here that I could think of nothing but a mess of nonsense. But to begin . . . as far as the city of Annapolis is concerned there is but little to be said. It is a small antiquated city which if it grows any, it is downhill. The only place of interest in it is the State House which contains the room in which General Washington resigned his commission as commander in chief of the U. S. Army. I am told that it is preserved as it was at the time of the resignation.

The grounds of the Academy are bounded on two sides by the Severn River or rather an arm of the Chesapeake Bay. On the other sides it is surrounded by a wall 15 feet high. The grounds (35 acres) are regularly laid out and well-shaded by trees. The grounds are lit by gas. The quarters of the students are situated on one side next to the Battery, while on the other side are the residences of the officers and professors. The buildings are all lit by gas and warmed by steam as the ship will soon be as the pipes are laid. Taken all together a person could hardly ask for a pleasanter place than it is on shore. How do you suppose it is on board ship? Not quite so pleasant as it is on shore yet not so unpleasant as to be unbearable. There are about 100 middies on board and these taken with the officers, seamen and waiters makes about 150 persons. I will give you a synopsis of the way I pass my time and you can judge for yourself. At 6 am the order comes to "turn out and lash your hammock." We are allowed one hour to do this, to wash, to dress, and to muster for inspection. At 7 the boatswain's whistle pipes us down to mess, after which we have until 8 to do what we please except 10 minutes for prayers. From eight until one p.m. is recitation or study hours. At 1 we are piped down to mess. At 2 we commence study or recitations until 4 when we go to drill at great guns, small arms, reefing and furling sails or knotting and splicing until 5 when it is muster and then comes mess again and until 6½ we have to ourselves, when we go to study until 9½ when we turn in for the night. This constitutes the program for the day. Not hard is it! Do not suppose when I tell you of our exercising with great guns that we actually fire them, for we do not. We merely go through all of the maneuvering and imagine we're firing. When we get so that we can manage a gun properly we will be allowed to practice firing. There is target shooting every Saturday from the battery by those who are ashore. . . . The size of the target is two yards square and has to be hit every time or the firer gets hissed. We are allowed to go ashore every Saturday and once every two weeks are allowed to go into town.

I could go on from page to page with a description of things which are new to me and doubtless to you but time forbids. Here at the South near the noted Harpers Ferry very little is said about it—not half as much as at the North. Niggers are as plenty as blackberries and as black too. Give my love to all. Write soon and write all of the news and believe me,

Your affectionate brother,
O. A. Batcheller
Acting Midshipman

NAVAL ACADEMY DECEMBER 4 1860

My dear Parents

. . . Congress met today but I have not been able to learn any of their proceedings but I suppose we shall soon know whether we are to have a union or not. For my part I think it rather doubtful, but time alone can tell. All the banks have suspended specie payments and I have it from a reliable source that the Secretary of the Treasury will not acknowledge any claims against the U.S. At all events the officers here have not been able to draw their last month's pay because the monthly requisition of the Purser (amounting to about $50,000) was not honored.

But be all this as it may there is only one course for us to pursue and that is to wait patiently the issue and then act as circumstances dictate. Dissolution must now be looked at as something more than a possibility—and I would like your advice as to how I shall act in that event, as you know it can do no hurt to be prepared.

Give my love to all and believe me as ever,

Your affectionate son,
O. A. Batcheller

NAVAL ACADEMY DECEMBER 9 1860

My dear Mother,

I improve this opportunity of writing you again hoping that this will find you enjoying the same good health that it leaves me in. I hardly know what to write—and perhaps I had better not write at all but I conceive it to be my duty to give you and father my opinion regarding my situation. You will, of course, take into consideration the fact that it is only my opinion and as such very liable to be wrong. It is the general idea here among officers and midshipmen that the Academy is going to be discontinued, or to use the common expression "bust up," whether the Union be dissolved or not. I have ridiculed the idea as absurd but I am forced to believe that there is ground for the report. Even if the Union is not immediately dissolved, the Academy must be stopped for the want of funds to carry it on with. I wrote John not long since that I heard that Captain Blake said that there would be no Academy here in two months, but I did not then think there was any foundation for such an assertion, but I am now compelled to look upon it as quite probable.

I may be entirely wrong. I hope I am, but it looks dark to me.

I can see no way to prevent the dissolution of the Union. The South demands concessions that the North cannot with honor make and therefore will not make. But I am telling you what you already know.

I hope the Union may not be dissolved and that the Naval Academy may continue to flourish, but as it is you need not be surprised to see me home ere long.

You can do as you choose about circulating what I have said among the gossips of Edinburgh as they are very apt to exaggerate everything that passes through their hands, but I think you will not blame me for making, to you, a statement of my opinion.

Love to all

Your affectionate son,

O. A. Batcheller

NAVAL ACADEMY DECEMBER 12TH

My dear Parents,

I read your kind note in due time and was very happy indeed to hear from you again and to know that you are well and flourishing. Nothing could give me greater pleasure than to occupy that spare seat you speak of at your table and I almost wish the Union might be dissolved so that I could do so.

Speaking of the dissolution of the Union, remind me of my foolishness in saying anything about it in my last, as I might have known that it would have caused you uneasiness and perhaps not do any good. But as I have commenced I may as well go on. What I wanted to get at is simply this: whether you thought I had better (in case the Union should be dissolved) step one side and wait for quieter times or take a part in the events as they transpire. Or in other words come home and keep quiet or take a part in the disturbance which is sure to follow dissolution. My last letter will give you something more of an idea of what I meant. Things look a little brighter than they did then, but even now I do not see any way to prevent, at the least, suspension of the Academy for a time. Should the Academy be only suspended I shall come home immediately.

I am afraid that I made matters look more serious to you than they really are but from all I could learn at that time I expected to see the Union dissolved very soon. All I wanted your advice on was as to how I should act in that event as I did not want to do anything without your sanction.

I only wish Buchanan had the courage to meet the emergency and to use his authority in keeping those states in the Union. If he had we might have an opportunity to exercise ourselves a little.

I am sorry to hear that this crisis has interfered with your business but I trust it will only be temporary and that you will be able to go on as usual soon. I regret to hear that Cousin Shaw is dead. It is indeed a serious loss to them. I sincerely hope that I may see Uncle Samuel this week as I can tell him what I mean so much better than I can write it.

Give my love to all and believe me

Yours affectionately

O. A. Batcheller

NAVAL ACADEMY JANUARY 1861

My dear Mother,

I'm too lazy to study this evening so I will answer your last, which I received today, in preference to doing nothing and I will answer each of your questions in the order they were asked, so I shall be sure to get them all.

In the first place I am, very well indeed, today, but so far from being a cold day it is quite the reverse, being very mild and pleasant and I am quite comfortable, sitting by the open window. I hardly think now that I shall be home before June, as the Navy appropriation bill has passed and there is money enough to carry on the School with. The only thing that I can see now that will break up the school is the secession of Virginia for if she goes out, Maryland will have to go too and then, of course, the Academy will be ended for a time at least. However, I don't think there is much prospect of this just now.

I guess John has over-reached my meaning a little in saying that I am going to fight the South if the Academy breaks up. I only said or at least I only meant that in case of Civil War, I would serve the North in any capacity provided my obligations to the Navy were cancelled beforehand.

I sincerely hope there will be no occasion for fighting for civil war is a terrible thing and ought to be avoided if possible, but it makes my blood boil to think that our flag should be fired on by a parcel of traitors and we compelled, through the imbecility or inability of the President, to pocket the insult. But never mind. Things must change after the 4th of March.

Give my love to all. Remember me kindly to Mr. Pease. Tell Father that although you write very well in his place, a line from him would be very acceptable.

Your obedient son,
O. A. Batcheller

NAVAL ACADEMY JANUARY 9, 1861
My dear brother,

The crisis approaches. The collision between government and the South Carolinians has doubtless taken place ere this and if it has, the time for decisive actions on the part of the government has come and if government fails to take the necessary measures, it falls upon the North to do so and I for one am for its assuming the responsibility of chastising the South if the Government will not do it. I believe the day of compromises is past and that if the Union is preserved it must be done by force. Buchanan seems to have gotten his eyes open at last and is acting with something like decision, but I fear that he has not got the moral force to meet the emergency. At all events, I think that independent of the struggle between government and the South there will be one between North and South and that the best thing that the North can do is to prepare for it by forming volunteer military companies to act by themselves or to cooperate with Government as circumstances may direct. As soon as my connection with the Navy is dissolved—and that will be soon I think—I am ready to serve in any capacity in the Army of the North. Governor Morgan represents N.Y. as able to take care of herself so far as means of defense is concerned, she having a militia of nearly 500,000 men. That is not a bad show and is of itself enough to crush a half dozen southern states.

Florida is out and Alabama, Mississippi and several others will doubtless be soon. Major Anderson has been reinforced by 250 men or at least they have been sent to him and if they manage to land at Fort Sumter, he will be safe. Mayor Wood—that disgrace to the city, state, and humanity, recommends the secession of the city from the state. He will be older than he is now before he sees that.

You must excuse me for not writing sooner for I have been and am very busy preparing for the February examinations. I am as well as usual and am getting along very well. Give my love to all and believe me

Your affectionate brother,
O. A. Batcheller

NAVAL ACADEMY SUNDAY JANUARY 13 1861
My dear Mother,

I received your kind note in due time and was happy to hear from you again. It does me good to hear from you and you need not fear but I will take your advice and "come home if I can," whether I can or not is another question. The excitement is intense here; numbers are resigning almost every day and everything is uncertain enough.

I think from what I see going on here that the Constitution—the schoolship—has been ordered to prepare for sea. She has been provisioned and watered for a hundred days and all the powder, etc. has been taken from the magazine of the Battery and placed on board her. Every thing has been done very quietly and no one knows (except the officers) what is going to be done. The Howitzers and Field piece muskets—and ball cartridges—that were in the Battery and Armory have also been taken on board ship. This, I think, is to guard against the possibility of the people of Annapolis rising and seizing them. There is a steamer, I understand, expected from Washington, Navy Yard, with the remainder of the Constitution's armament, she not having more than half her number of guns now. The only question of interest to me in all this is this: Are we going to sea with the Constitution if she goes? I would like to have this question answered if possible but I see no prospect of it just now. It would be, in some respects, very pleasant to go with her, but in others it would not be so pleasant. Taking it all together, I had quite as soon not go as to go in the capacity that I would have to go in. I would jump at the chance of going to sea and doing midshipman duties, but as for being bundled on board the ship with two hundred others and having to do duty as a man and not as an officer, I beg to be excused. This is the mind of nearly every one here.

Of course, no one who knows nothing of the case would say that our not wanting to go to sea in the Constitution is anything but complimentary to us, but I don't care for that. I did not enter the service to do man's duty "before the mast" and I don't mean to do it now if I can help it.

Of course, I say this to you and father and not anyone and every one who has the curiosity to inquire of you what is going on here.

I shall write to you again in a day or two and perhaps I can then tell you more about this; at all events don't be at all alarmed as it may all be a hoax. I shall keep you all posted on any change that may take place here. Give my love to all and believe me

Your affectionate son
O. A. Batcheller

NAVAL ACADEMY FEBRUARY 21, 1861

My dear Parents,

Again I take up my pen to improve this spare hour in writing you a few lines. My spare hours are not as plenty as I could wish but I suppose you would not care to have them more if you were to be bored with a letter for every one of them.

I am as well as usual in every respect. My health, if possible, is better than it was a month ago, as I then had a slight cold, which is now entirely gone. The weather is fine now-adays; almost like spring. The grass is beginning to grow and the buds of the trees to open. In fact, everything but the cold nights is exactly like spring.

We received a visit today from the son of President Lincoln. He came here with a nephew of Major Anderson from Harvard University to see a friend of his. He is rather a fine looking young man and if he at all resembles his father, I can see nothing which could render either of them ugly.

Nothing worthy of note has transpired here lately except the addition of a few 32 pounders to the armament of the Academy, but these have long been needed, as some of those we have had were condemned and only used for firing salutes, so we can attach no importance to it.

The usual National salute was fired here on the 22nd but no further observation was taken of the day in the Yard or the town.

It is much feared that the "Peace Conference" will adjourn without affecting the purpose for which it was conceived. There was a rumor yesterday that a modification of the border state resolutions had been adopted but today's papers destroy that illusion and we are left just where we were.

The South Carolinians say that Fort Sumter will be attacked unless Mr. Lincoln's inaugural speech is conservative and judging from the preparations they have made, I think they will do so: but whether they succeed or not is for Major Anderson to decide. My time is up and I must close. Give my love to all and believe me

Your obedient son.

O. A. Batcheller

U.S NAVAL ACADEMY MARCH 6, 1861

My dear Mother,

Yours of the 28th with enclosed money was received in due time; and for which accept my sincere thanks.

You were right in thinking that I would not have sent for it unless it had been necessary and you did me a great favor in sending it when you did as I had deferred asking for it until the last moment, hoping to get along without it.

We have been having very warm weather here for the past two or three days: so warm in fact that the leaves are beginning to start very finely.

You have doubtless heard ere this of the peaceable inauguration of Mr. Lincoln and of his inaugural speech. It seems to be the general impression hereabouts that this will be immediately followed by the secession of Virginia and Maryland as he seems to advocate coercion rather strongly. I have deduced so many consequences from secession that I perhaps had better say no more about it but I will say this. In my opinion the prospect of this Academy is darker than it has been at any time yet, for if Virginia secedes Maryland will go and with her goes the Academy.

Everything depends on the actions of these two states and as Virginia is in convention now, I will not say anymore until I hear from her.

Your affectionate son,
O. A. Batcheller

NAVAL ACADEMY APRIL 7 1861

"Mon cher Frere"

I improve this opportunity of adding a little to my last which was so brief. I am, as you will see by the date of this, back in my old quarters again, running my "machine"— "studying machine"—again as usual and hope to be able to continue to do so until the time shall come for books to be laid aside and for study to go to the dogs.

I am as well as I was before I was sick and I think that I can study better for my rest: at least I don't think that I lost anything but a few pounds of flesh and that I can spare without inconvenience.

I sincerely hope that you may have a good year for farming so that you may be able to clear your farm from incumbrances and I wish that I was in a condition to assist you. I have $100.00 in the Treasury and will have $100 more for each year or $300 when I graduate. That will be of no use to me until then, but the worst of it is I cannot control it until then or you might have it. This $100 a year is reserved from our pay of $500 a year for the purpose of purchasing our outfit when we shall graduate. A complete outfit for a two years cruise will cost from $300 to $500.

It seems to me that political affairs will soon be brought to a crisis by the movements which the Administration is now making. Either one or the other has got to back down or there must be war. The South must consent to have those forts reinforced or the Administration must abandon its attempts to reinforce them or war will be the result.

I am rather pleased than not at the policy which these military and naval movements foreshadow. It is just what I expected from the Administration. I was bitterly disappointed when I heard that Fort Sumter was to be evacuated, as I looked upon it as a virtual renunciation of all the North has claimed and fought for, for years: but I think now that there is no intention of evacuating it and that rumor was only a strategem to gain time.

Old Seward has got a long head and knows very well what he is about. He is the virtual head of the Administration and the interests of the Republicans will not suffer in his hands. What a pity it is that he could not have been elected President instead of Lincoln, who is doubtless a very able and worthy man but he has done so little for the party while Seward has done so much. However we can hope to see justice done to New York's favorite son in 1864. I believe that the whole Administration is made up of men who will "stand up to the rack fodder or no fodder" and who will not flinch a hair from responsibility. Besides this they are supported by the ministers of all the considerable powers of Europe, who say that their governments will not recognize any "Southern Confederacy" and will support the Administration in any policy which it may pursue towards the seceding States. Spain only is willing to recognize their independence and we are on the eve of war with her anyway.

But the drum is beating for chapel and I must close. Give my love to all and believe me your

Affectionate Brother
O. A. Batcheller

NAVAL ACADEMY APRIL 12 1861
My dear Parents

I improve the free leisure moments which I have this evening in writing you a few lines informing you of my continued good health.

I have not heard from you this week but I suppose that you are all well nevertheless. I received two notes in quick succession from Belle last week concerning photographs, etc, which are all right as it would not be possible for me to go to Baltimore anyway. I am glad that you are pleased with those which I sent you of the Academy. They are very good pictures and will give you a pretty good idea of what kind of a place it is here.

I think that Uncle Samuel will recognize most of them and will be able to explain them to you: you did not say whether they were in a good condition or not. I had some doubts about sending them at all for fear they might be injured on the way. I hope that they were not. It will cost so much to get them all nicely framed that I hardly think it would be best to do so at present.

There is considerable excitement here concerning the military and naval movements which are now being made and there are a thousand and one rumors afloat all of which are, perhaps, wrong. One thing, however, is certain. That is that immense Naval and land forces are being collected on our Southern coast, but where no one knows, probably off Charleston.

Vessels which have laid in "ordinary" for years are now being fitted out in the greatest haste. . . .

It is thought that the present 1st class will be graduated immediately and ordered to the vessels which are now being fitted out. If this be the case it will probably shorten our course here one term—4 months—and perhaps deprive us of our leave of absence.

Great excitement prevails at Washington and it is proposed to declare martial law. The militia is being sworn in and great care is taken to select only those who are known to be firm union men, the oath being refused to all who are in any ways doubtful.

What the result of all this will be is of course only to be guessed, but I think that we will find out that there is someone who has more energy than Buchanan at the head of affairs.

Give my love to all and believe me as ever

Your affectionate son,

O. A. Batcheller

NAVAL ACADEMY APRIL 18 1861

My dear Parents,

Having a few moments this afternoon I improve them by writing you a few lines thinking they might be acceptable in view of the present state of affairs.

The excitement here is intense, and study with most all of us has been laid aside for the present. I, however, study a little just to keep my hand in. The guns, shot, shell, powder, etc. have been taken from the Battery and placed on board the Constitution for safe keeping I suppose. Today's paper says that the Constitution will heave up her anchors and drop down the channel a little farther where she will lay for the purpose of protecting the Academy, etc. The rumor concerning the graduation of the 1st class is officially confirmed. The examination is to commence in a few days.

There is a rumor afloat concerning the removal of the Naval Academy to Fort Adams, near Newport, R. I. but I do not credit it though I hope it is so. It would be much more pleasant if we could have the Academy upon Northern soil, as the Military Academy is, where we could be near those who think and feel as we do and where we might speak our minds without fear of wounding the delicate feelings of those who live by the institution of slavery. However, the Academy is likely to be rid of those who do not wish for the success of our flag or the life of our government, as it seems to be the policy of the Administration to dismiss all who wish to resign just now, and most of the Southerners have tendered their resignations.

I am tired of this sort of life and wish that it might be changed. There is now a chance for active service—a good chance—and we cannot have an opportunity of improving it. I wish they would break up the Academy, put us on board the different ships now fitting out or already fitted out and let us wade in to the Southern Confederacy to our hearts content.

I have commenced giving up all thoughts of leave this summer as I think the chances of our getting it are so slim that I shall only be disappointed if I think of it at all, so I have commenced early to forget all about it. (I don't succeed very well)

I forgot to say in its proper place that it is probable that we will have to mount guard around the Yard soon. There is an armed guard kept on board the Constitution. Her guns are all shotted. Our muskets in the armory are all supplied with ball cartridges, and in short every precaution possible is taken to guard against surprise.

My time is up and I must close. Give my best love to all and believe me

Your obedient son
O. A. Batcheller

NAVAL ACADEMY APRIL 19 1861

Dear Father,

The excitement which, as I wrote you in my last letter, has prevailed here since the bombardment of Fort Sumter, reached its highest pitch last night when information was received of a contemplated attack upon the Academy by the secessionists of Maryland. The information was received from a reliable source and was confirmed by many suspicious circumstances, such as signal lights appearing and disappearing along the river and harbor and boats moving around where they could have no possible business except to reconnoiter.

These circumstances were seen and noted before the definite information was received of the designed attack and it was thought sufficient to keep a good watch on them: but when that information was received it was at once determined to mount the guard and prepare to defend the exposed points. Accordingly one company of infantry and three of artillery were detailed for this duty.

I had turned in at 10 P.M. thinking there would be nothing done and had just fallen asleep when I was called and told to dress as soon as possible. Hastily dressing myself I repaired to the Armory, where I found a crowd arming themselves and following their example I was soon armed in the following style: a revolver in my belt, a broad sword at my side, and a musket on my shoulder, quite ready to travel around the Yard for 8 hours, if nothing more.

The howitzers were planted in the most favorable position, the guards stationed at regular intervals around the Yard and the night passed without interruption.

The latest news confirms the rumor of Virginia's having seceded but leaves everything concerning the Norfolk Navy Yard in doubt. It is much to be hoped that the Yard has not been seized for it will be a serious loss to us and an important item to them.

The vessels there can be of no possible use to them as the Yard is so situated that they cannot be taken out without passing directly under the guns of the Fortress Monroe by which they would be sunk in no time, but the munitions of war, of which there are great quantities there, will be of great use to them. There is or at least there was when I was there, about fifty tons of powder, between two and three thousand pieces of ordnance—old and new together—and a corresponding quantity of shot and shell besides a vast amount of timbre for ship building. . . .

I think that if there was anything wanted to raise the spirits of the North up to fighting pitch, this last outrage, the secret secession of Virginia, the seizure or attempted seizure of Norfolk and the sinking of light boats in the channel of Hampton Roads, is enough, and more than enough to do it, and adding to it the assaulting of volunteer troops as they passed through Baltimore. It is positively unbearable.

I am very glad to see how promptly the North has responded to the call for volunteers and I hope that the same spirit will continue to prevail until every insult which our flag and government have received shall be wiped out with blood. The time for deliberation is past and nothing but prompt and decisive action will suit the times. Hesitation on the part of anyone is treason now and ought to be punished as such. Had it not been for the hesitating, wavering, timorous policy of Buchanan, the stars and stripes might still have waved over Sumter and instead of having given aid and assistance to traitors, government would now have had its foot upon their necks. But enough of this.

Love to all

Your obedient son,

O. A. Batcheller

US FRIGATE CONSTITUTION AT SEA APRIL 28 1861

Dear Parents,

I improve this opportunity of writing you a few lines thinking they will be acceptable when they reach you, as they will inform you of my whereabouts and of my continued good health.

We left the Academy Thursday evening on the steam tug Josephine which took us to the Constitution, then lying off Annapolis Road and on Friday morning we got underway. . . .

We were compelled to leave the Academy by its being turned into a temporary Military Station for the reception of troops bound South. I was very sorry to leave it under such circumstances and I think that such was the feeling of nearly everyone attached to the school. Indeed I never saw a more affecting sight than it was when we left. We were formed in lines to be marched to the wharf where we were to embark. Captain Rogers came out and attempted to say something to us but was so much affected that he could only say "prove true to the flag! prove true to the flag! God Bless You all!" There was not a dry eye in the crowd and even among the soldiers there were many who were deeply affected. When the band struck up a national air, the cry went out "Three cheers for the Midshipmen" and such cheering I never heard before. There were about 4000 troops in the Yard and each seemed bound to cheer as loud as he could, and all the way to the wharf it was one continual cheer, cheer, cheer.

We are now pretty well on our way to New York and if we have good luck we will be there before dark. Where we are to go after our arrival there is unknown. Perhaps to sea; perhaps on leave; or perhaps there will be a temporary Academy fitted up in which we will continue our studies. Probably one of these three things will be done, but which no one knows. For myself, I have but one choice and that is to go to sea, as it is there and only there that I can have an opportunity of doing what I wish—seeing actual service.

Probably we will receive orders to do something soon after our arrival in port and should it be to remain there for any length of time I would like very much to see some one of you there if only for a day or two. However, I will write you more on this subject before long. At present I can only subscribe myself,

Your obedient son,
O. A. Batcheller

CHAPTER 4

War Is Inevitable

The Letters of Philip Henry Cooper

"The first blow has been struck by the South and it will not end there." The year was 1861 and the young Philip Henry Cooper had just learned of the Confederate attack on Fort Sumter.

Housed on the Constitution, *which had replaced the* Plymouth *as a school ship, Cooper and his classmates did not know what to expect. Before the war, Cooper described a comfortable routine: "At night we have to sleep on hammocks slung upon the berthdeck" and "Every Saturday morning we have a band on board and have a dance for two hours on the quarter deck." But the dancing stopped with the attack on Fort Sumter. After the* Constitution *sailed to Newport, Cooper warned his family: "There is every chance of our class being ordered to sea. . . . If I do go I hope all of you may pray for my safety for if I am ordered into the home squadron or the blockading fleet, I shall see some warm times."*

Cooper was right. His class was called into active duty in 1863. This Camden, New York, native fought bravely in the Civil War. In time, Cooper returned to Annapolis to serve as superintendent of the Naval Academy from November 1894 until July 1898. He retired in 1904 as a rear admiral.

ON BOARD SCHOOL SHIP CONSTITUTION ANNAPOLIS
SUNDAY SEPTEMBER 30, 1860
My Dear Mother,

I guess you will think that I have nearly forgotten you, but I have been so busy that I have had no time. You can believe that I am homesick and would start tonight if I could. It is so different from what I have ever been used to living. I arrived here on Friday and was examined before the Medical Board in the morning where I had to take off all my clothes entirely naked and I passed that without any difficulty. And in the afternoon was examined before a board of professors which I also passed. Yesterday I went to the Secretary of the Academy to make my deposit and get an order for my outfit, which was a great cost to me. I have got to raise 36 dollars more for which I will send you a certificate from the Secretary.

My outfit was $44 to which there is to be made a deposit of $50 besides, making $94. Then from this the travelling expenses were taken which were $10, leaving $76 which I would have to give him but I handed him $39 leaving $36 to be paid back. The Pay in the school is $500 a year, but this is not given to us until graduation, except a dollar a month for spending. But if I want anything I have to go to the Store in the Academy Yard and it is charged to your account or if I want to send a letter I hand it to the messenger and the stamp is charged. As soon as I passed I was put on board the school ship with a hundred others. They are divided into Crews of a certain number in each which have to muster on the deck for everything—as going to meals or going to study rooms, etc.

At night we have to sleep on hammocks slung upon the berthdeck. We have to go to bed at 9:30 and get up at 6. I forgot to say that our board is $13 a month and our washing is $1. I wish I stayed home now for there is nothing like having a Father's and a Mother's care and love. I wish I could go tomorrow. If you cannot raise the money, write to Mr. Heath or some of them and send the Certificate to them and then if the money is not raised, next month I will get money some way and start for home. We have an examination in February, and if we do not pass we are sent into the same class and next June we are examined again. And if they do not pass they are sent home and paid off. But if they do, they are sent on a cruise of three months to the Mediterranean and when they get back are put in the Academy on shore for 3 years.

Have you heard from Pa yet? O how I want to see him. He must come down here when he comes home and bring you with him. Give my love to him and tell him that I have got into the Navy and how I am doing

Philip Henry Cooper *Courtesy USNA Nimitz Special Collections*

and I will write to him if you think he will get it before he starts for home. Send me his letters and you and Emma and the rest must write to me very often for I am very home sick. I met Fred and some others on board the Newton and we had a fine time. If I could only have seen Pa before I started I should have felt better. He is so far off. We cannot get off only once in two weeks and then for only a few hours. Give my love to all and do not think I can ever forget you, but instead of that I shall be closer and closer drawn to all of you. I shall try to get twenty dollars of my own and send it to him if I can in a short time. You want to send me 4 pairs of drawers and some shirts and collars, if you can sometime before winter.

Oceans of love to you all. I will write again soon and send that Certificate I spoke of. If you cannot raise it why I will try to get all that is credited to me and go back. Write often. Directions on the back.

Your son,
Philip

US SHIP CONSTITUTION SUNDAY OCTOBER 14TH
3 O CLOCK PM

My Dear Parents,

I received a letter from you Wednesday and answered it the same day but I am going to try to write a little more. I expect it will be long enough to make up for the short ones that I have got. I should like to take a peep into the house today to see how you are all placed. It would be the grandest sight for me in the world. I expect that Pa is sleeping about this time. It is study hours now and I am at the desk in section room No. 3 on the Starboard side of the ship on the Gundeck or the second one. On Sunday we have study hours from 3 to 4 and from 7:30 to 9:15 to make up for Saturday afternoon and evening when we have liberty. One half of the Gun Crews go out into the town and the other half stay in the Yard. I went out into the city yesterday afternoon for the first time in two weeks. I went to the old State House where Washington resigned his commission, as President. The room remains exactly the same as it was at that time with the exception of some paintings, and I see a painting of Washington was executed by Rembrandt Peale's father in the time of the Revolution just before some great battle, and they have all the original copies of the laws ever since the State was organized and a great many relics of bygone days.

I was surprised when I came to this place. I thought I was going to see some grand sight but instead I found the dullest town in the United States. There is no business going on. I have not seen three horses. It is a great deal worse than Cape Vincent or the Manor. All the residences there are, are those of Academy officers in the Yard. The buildings in the town are old tumble down rookeries built in 1700.

Every Saturday morning we have a band on board and have a dance for two hours on the quarter deck and on Sunday we have religious exercises by a Chaplain from the Yard. The service is Episcopalian. Everyone is obliged to be present. I wish you could come so as to be here on Saturday and Sunday. I should have more time to spare then. Ask Emma why she does not write to me. She has a great deal of time to spare and can do it if she chooses I know. Do you think you will go to Texas before spring? If you do not, I may be ready to go with you by that time. I want to stay long enough to earn enough money sufficient to get an outfit to start with. I wish you could get a place in N.Y. I should be glad to stay here. If you could get a good mill in the state somewhere, I should like it. Why do you not look around and see what there is. . . . I wait impatiently for another letter.

Your ever loving son,
Philip

US FRIGATE CONSTITUTION   OCTOBER 21ST

My Dear Parents,

I received two letters from you this week and have not had the opportunity to answer until now.

The Mids think I have got the most excellent parents in the world to write to me so often. I do wish that I could see you all at home but you must not think that I am downhearted for I am not. I am doing finely and am enjoying myself. In my classes I am getting along finely and stand well. There has been a change in the whole class. They have been arranged in new sections according to merit. Each study is made up into 8 sections. The best in standing are placed in the highest sections. The highest merit or average for the month is 4. In Arithmetic I am in the 2d section or No. 23 in the whole school on board ship, with a merit of 3.25 and probably one half of those above me are no better than I am. In Grammar I am in the 3rd with an average of 3.05. So you see I am standing well and have a good chance to pass although I have got to study awful hard to keep up in my sections, which I shall try to do. There is a change once a month. I anticipate a happy future if I do not get homesick and get backward in my studies. If you do not do well, I shall worry myself so that I will lose my position. I wish you were settled in a grand good position in New York state. I should be happy. In two years or nearly that you will see me coming home in full uniform with a warrant in my pocket as a Midshipman. There is one of the finest men in the Navy placed in command on board ship and he takes all the care and pride in the class. He says that we know more about seamanship than a great many others that have been here for three months. My station at the Gun is 2nd Shotman and 1st Pumpman and my station aloft is in the Starboard watch on the Main Yard. I have got so that I am very much at home on the ship and am fascinated with the life, but I think I have said enough about myself.

You speak of having some pictures of me in full length. In a short time I shall have a lot of splendid photographs of the Academy buildings and the ship consisting of 12 large and 10 small ones and then I shall have 6 of myself taken. They are one dollar for the first and 25 cents for the impressions each. Just as good a picture as you can get in Albany for 3 dollars.

When do you think you will come and see me. After you get to New York you take the Newark Road to Philadelphia. The fare will be 3 dollars and from Philadelphia to Baltimore will be 3 dollars more paying all the ferry fare—besides you have to cross the river 3 or 4 times and from Baltimore to Annapolis it is one dollar. I can not tell what the Hotel bill will be. You must bring as little baggage as possible for it costs an awful sight for hack fare. I shall write to you every Sunday and Wednesday which are the only days I can get time. I have joined a Bible class on board and that will take more of my spare time. . . . I will write again soon.

From your loving Son,
Philip

US SHIP CONSTITUTION OCTOBER 28TH 1860 SUNDAY 2PM

My dear Parents,

What can be the matter with you all at home. I have not received a letter from you this week. I got some papers but not a written word have I got. I begin to get very anxious about you. It cannot be that a letter could have got lost or that you are sick. I wrote to you last Sunday and have been too busy to write since. I am so engaged in my studies and exercises that there is not time left to write. I should like to hear from you twice a week. I expect to hear very soon that you have got a place in New York State instead of going to Texas which news would be very welcome you can believe. It may be better for you to go to Texas but it is so far from the seaboard that it would be a very long way for one to go on leave after I have graduated, if I do. Do you think you will ever see me a Lieutenant? I have got it in my eye and shall look for it in a few years from now, if I live. But that is an office that only about 10 out of a hundred can reach. With my own talents and a Father's and a Mother's love and encouragement, I shall battle hard for it.

Captain Blake, the Superintendent, came on board this morning for Divine Service. He is a very nice looking old man indeed. He looks a great deal like Fennimore Cooper. He has a regular Cooper look about him, for which I can compliment myself.

Lt. Rodgers, the man that has charge of us on board is a very nice man. He does all he can to promote the welfare of each one of us. He is kinder and more obliging than a great many that they could put in that position. I wish you would bring that glass with you, that you gave me last spring, if you have got it. Was it in your trunk last spring when it was lost? It might be of some service to me. Did you ever hear from Uncle Henry and what is he doing? I joined a Bible class today on board ship. I have never been to Sunday school enough when I had the chance but am going to make up for it now. I have got to have my old teeth pulled this week and those that are unsound have got to be filled. You do not know how much I like this life. It suits to perfection. Rowing in boats, musket drill, Great Gun exercise, and Seamanship. I hope I shall never give it up without I am obliged to.

We are having practice in crossing Yards now for a short time. The other day I was sent aloft to learn how to do it. I was stationed on the Crosstrees—not the first landing but the next above it. It is fun alive to get way up there and out on the yards and running all over the ship. It is so much better than being a clerk in a store or anything of that sort. Tell the children and Emma that I have not heard a word from them yet. I do not think they do right in neglecting me. It is a very small job for them to sit down and write a few words to me.

Enclosed you will find a list of the studies of the four classes and Midshipmen that are sent from sea to study here. You can easily see how it reads. It is something I dress off on purpose to send to you. I wish you would send my skates, too, for there is a few weeks that they have ice here and then there is sport. It is almost as warm as our summer north now.

7:30 PM

I have just got through the worst job we have—that is I have got my hammock lashed and ready to turn in which will be at 9:30. From this time until then we have to study our lessons for Monday. Last night at our dance there were about 30 ladies came on and several of the officers from the shore. There are some of the handsomest young ladies here that can ever be seen in such a small place as this. It pleases the Mids very much to have them come on board for it is very seldom that they can see one. When you come here, inquire for the City Hotel and when you get there, tell them that you have a son on the Constitution. They will send a little nigger boy with you and when you get on board inquire for me and any of them will bring you to me. I shall expect to see you before long, both of you, but do not come until you decide what you are going to do. I wish you could answer this very prompt for I am anxious to hear from home. Tell me if you have written last week. Give my love to all reserving great quantities for yourselves. I shall write again in a few days. Tell Emma that I hope to get a letter from her soon. . . .

Your son,
Philip

USS CONSTITUTION JANUARY 20, 1861

My Dear Parents,

I have not yet received a letter from you but I am waiting patiently. I cannot believe but that you arrived safe. I hope I shall not have to wait more than two or three days. If I were only with you I should feel content but it may be a long time before I shall see you. My first letter may be lost, the one in which I asked your leave to come home. This is the fourth that I have written since you have been gone. I am so anxious to know how you are and how well contented you are with the country that I can hardly sleep nights for thinking of you. I have not been quite as homesick lately as I was at first. There is so much to occupy my time, getting ready for examinations and the stirring times there are in the country and as I am so well assured that you will send for me, I do not think so much. I hope you like it in Texas for it is the best thing in the world that you have left this country when you did. We are going to have hard times. War is inevitable. In less than two months we will be fighting hard. The first blow has been struck by the South and it will not end there. There will be a great deal of suffering and many lives lost before this trouble is ended. South Carolina, Florida, Alabama, Mississippi, and Georgia have already left the Union and before the end of February the remainder of the Southern states will be out. All of the forts, arsenals, besides other government property have been seized with the exception of a few of the strongest. They are recruiting large bodies of troops and making great preparations for a hard and bloody war. Fort Sumter, the most impregnable fortress in the South, is situated in Charleston harbor. It is commanded by a brave officer by the name of

Major Anderson with a force of 79 men, who left the other fortifications in the harbor and took possession of this. The President with the Cabinet concluded to reinforce Major Anderson. Accordingly General Scott, who is acting Secretary of War, chartered a mail steamer in New York called the Star of the West, and put aboard her 250 troops and provisions from Governors Island and sent them to Charleston. On the morning of the 9th of January she arrived off Charleston Bar and attempted to enter the harbor with the American Flag flying when a brisk fire was opened on her. . . . She being manned, was unable to stand this, consequently she put about and went to sea and put back for New York. Major Anderson from Fort Sumter did not return the fire as he had no orders from the government to do so. Since then The Republic of South Carolina sent an ambassador to Washington and demanded the unconditional surrender of Fort Sumter. This was refused and dispatches were sent to Major Anderson to defend the fort to the last. We expect to hear everyday that an attack has been made on the fort. It can not be taken with a loss less than 10,000 men. The very moment that this occurs a fleet will be sent to blockade Charleston, and the city will be laid in ashes. Governor Morgan of New York with the Senate offered the state militia to the President as well as money and provisions. The Governors of all others of the States which are true to the Union have done the same. The Mayor in his message to the Common Council advises the secession of the city from the state and make it a free city and appoint him governor. If there are any spoils to be made, he will surely have his hand in them. He ought to be rode on a rail. I don't suppose you hear much of the events of this part of the country. Before you receive this Texas will probably be out of the Union and the Lone Star Flag will once more float. It will make no difference with you as you are situated. When you get my next letter you will most likely hear one of three things. Either that the school is removed to some northern state or that we are all at sea or that it is broken up and I am working for money to get home with, or you may see me instead of getting a letter. If I get the money from you, I shall most assuredly start for Texas with a good rifle and my effects for the ones I love. Love is not the word for it. Something stronger must be used. Many is the day I hope to pass on the plains and mountains of Texas. I should like to see some fighting first and there is a great chance of it too. We may be attacked here by the mob if Maryland should secede, as she certainly will, but we are well prepared for defense. If they could get such a ship as this in their power they might consider themselves well off, but the honor and glory of Old Ironsides must be defended with the last drop of American blood and before the treasonists to our country will get her, we will blow her out of the water. Next to parents, brothers and sisters, I love this old ship. I do really hope that Texas will suit you for I do not want you to come back until everything is at peace and not until you are wealthy enough to live in good style. Is there any danger of the Indians where you are? In case of a general war, they are the only things you have to fear. As soon as Old Abe takes the chair, matters will change. Buchanan has not the grit to carry the country through the storm. The Southerners are determined that Lincoln shall not be inaugurated and it is rumored that there is a secret organization to take the city of Washington and shoot Lincoln if he enters the city. But efforts have been equally strong on his part . . . there is to be a strong military guard in Washington and as sure as the 4th of March comes Abe will take his oath of office. I guess you will think that I am getting to be a strong politician but I cannot help it. . . .

May God bless you in your new home and give you success in your new undertaking and if I am destined to stay in the Navy, may I never do the least thing in word or action that will cause you to blush with shame for me. And I hope that the time may come when I can add glory to the name which I bear. I will finish for the present. Love to all. Write often to your

Son Philip

US FRIGATE CONSTITUTION OFF FORT ADAMS
NEWPORT RHODE ISLAND SUNDAY MAY 19TH 1861
My dear Parents, Brothers and Sisters,

You will be much surprised when you receive this letter and find where I am, but I have got some strange things to tell you before I finish.

You may be angry or feel hard because I have not written for so long a time but you will forgive me when I tell you my story: it is now nearly a month since I wrote you last. I received a letter from you last Sunday morning dated the 8th of April, which was very thankfully received for it has been a long time since I heard from you and I began to feel anxious for your safety.

You have most likely heard of the war which is now waging in this country between the government and some of the states which have rebelled and united themselves in what they call the Southern Confederacy with Jeff Davis as President and A. H. Steven as Vice. This rebellion has been premeditated long back by those who were highest in authority and they have finally brought it to a crisis, and there will be some hard fighting before they are brought back to rights. Those that are now in power are capable of doing it. They commenced the bombardment of Fort Sumter of which you have read in my letters. This fort was garrisoned with 79 men and the attacking party consisted of over 10,000 men with some of the most splendid batteries in the world and after a siege of two days and nights Major Anderson was obliged to surrender after doing the most terrible execution and his fort was on fire set by the hot shot of the secessionists, and they had eaten their last morsel two days before. This was the first conflict of the present war, nothing has been accurately ascertained with regard to the number killed for the means of information have mostly been in the hands of the rebels. Though there are gentlemen given their evidence as eyewitnesses of the fight that there were nearly 200 killed and a number wounded and one man, a captain of a schooner then in Charleston, states that he is willing to take his oath that at least 160 dead were carried on the deck of his vessel to Potters Field. It is certain that some must have been killed for the damage that was done by Major Anderson was terrific. As soon as intelligence of this reached Washington, the President made a proclamation calling out 75,000 militia and giving the persons in possession of public property in the seceded States twenty days to retire to their homes, peaceably and calling an extra session of Congress to meet on the 4th of July. Soon after he issued another proclamation calling out 42,000 militia and 23,000 regulars and

18,000 seamen. You have never seen such an uprising as there was at that time. There is but one sentiment in the North and that is for union and the support of the constitution. In less than two weeks there were enough troops enlisted to carry on the war, and it keeps so. The navy has increased greatly. All the vessels that were lying in the navy yard rotting, have been fitted for sea, new ones have been purchased and soon we will have a large navy. I forgot to state that the President in his proclamation declared the southern ports from the mouth of the James river in Virginia to the Rio Grande as under a strict blockade. This is the cause of the great increase of the navy. Some of the ports are under blockade now and before two weeks more, every port will be sealed tight. The twenty days are up now and I expect there will be some great moves made soon. I noticed by yesterday's papers that 800 secessionists were taken at St. Louis. Now to come nearer home. Soon after the fall of Fort Sumter matters appeared in Virginia and Maryland as if the secessionists at Norfolk were in great numbers and demonstrations were made against the Navy Yard there, where there were a number of vessels and a great and valuable quantity of naval stores and some splendid buildings. After a time it was found impossible to hold it, with the small force. Consequently, everything was destroyed. Ships were burnt and scuttled and only one escaped and that is the Cumberland steam frigate, which is now blocking the port of Norfolk and Hampton roads. She has already captured a large fleet of small craft which tried to run through. The whole Chesapeake is blockaded as well as the Potomac which constitutes the only means of the inland commerce of Virginia. Shortly before this affair at Norfolk, there had been a riot in Baltimore, which was but 25 miles from us, caused by the secessionists there. A body of troops were passing through and they were attacked by the mob with stones and fire arms which they had to return the fire in order to defend themselves. There were quite a number killed on both sides. From these circumstances and from the prevailing sentiment of the people, we were in great danger of an attack. The Constitution, we know, would be a great prize to them, and the buildings would be splendid barracks for their troops. Besides if they could hold Annapolis it would form a great rendezvous for their army.

There were at that time 76 midshipmen on the ship and 25 sailors besides the officers, including those on shore. We were put on strict guard duty night and day during this time. We were frequently called to quarters ready for a fight. Our guns were loaded with shot and shell and all the time each one was armed to the teeth, and for two weeks I never had my clothes off.

Things kept looking and growing worse until it was found impossible to keep the ship in place. The secessionists were around the ship in the day, noting her assailable points, and they could often be seen on the opposite shore, drilling. The ship drew more water than there was on the tar; consequently, they thought she was in their power, and they could take her as soon as they were in sufficient force. At length Saturday night the 20th of April, it was decided to take the ship out. The steamer Maryland coming up that night it was decided to use her to tow us out. This steamer had been seized in Havre de Grace for the purpose of transporting a regiment of volunteers to Annapolis.

At 7 A.M. Sunday the order was received to take the ship out, her mooring chains were slipped. One anchor was raised and we were under way at 9 o' clock. All the midshipmen had been sent on shore but 14 were chosen by the commander to act as officers of the ship, of which number I was one. After great difficulties and dangers we succeeded in getting the ship to the outer bar, when the captain of the steamer purposely ran the ship aground and backed his own steamer on the bar. He was instantly put under arrest and some of the soldiers ran the steamer. The reason that the captain acted in this manner was that the boat had been seized without his consent and he was a secessionist himself and would do as much harm as he possibly could. The steamer is now in the service of the government as a transport.

We dropped anchor and intended to stay there all night, but about 9 o clock Captain Blake sent word to us that he had been informed that it was the intention of the Secessionists to attack the ship and place obstructions in the channel outside of us, when immediately all hands were called to kedge the ship out. . . . We worked at this all night when early in the morning a steamer hove in sight bringing a bearer of dispatches.

This steamer took us in tow and carried us out to our anchorage ground in the bay. We stayed there Monday until Friday, during which time there were at least twenty thousand troops came up from Annapolis en route to Washington. They were brought in steamers which had been chartered by the government for the purpose. It was now found impossible to keep the Naval School at this place. Consequently, midshipmen were put on board the Constitution and Friday morning we sailed, bound for New York. . . . We had a splendid passage and Sunday night at 10 o clock we dropped anchor off the battery. I wish to say that I was not seasick at all during the trip. The next day we went to the Navy Yard where we anchored waiting orders from Washington. . . . Tuesday May 7th we received orders to sail to Newport where we arrived the next noon and where we are now anchored. . . . I may soon be called into active service and then it may be found out if I am capable of holding any office. I have every prospect of success in after life. I stand high in my class and I hope in the opinions of the officers who are over me, and have no enemies among my own classmates or among the classes senior to mine.

There is every chance of our class being ordered to sea. Three classes have been ordered to sea already, and there are some of our most prominent men now in Washington using their influence in that direction. I expect to tell you in my next letter that I am ordered to report to the commodore of the N. Y. Navy Yard for duty, and then of my orders for ship.

If I do go I hope all of you may pray for my safety for if I am ordered into the home squadron or the blockading fleet, I shall see some warm times. I shall pray for the welfare of my family and that the day may be soon that we are united. . . .

Your loving son and brother,
Philip

CHAPTER 5

Castor Oil in the Applesauce

The Letters of Harry Phelps

"Did they put castor oil in the applesauce?" Harry Phelps asked one of his friends during dinner on 11 October 1877. The question earned him demerits, as did another culinary offense on 29 January 1878. On that day he was disciplined for "bringing [an] orange to examination and eating it." But Phelps's offenses were nothing more than curious.

Phelps attended the academy when the school, like the Navy, struggled with its post–Civil War identity. His letters, however, do not bespeak any dissatisfaction with the diminished role of the Navy. With equal detail and energy he wrote of "a great storm here last Thursday," "a hop last Monday," and a "man in the fourth class called Jones."

Harry, who would rise to the rank of commodore before he retired in 1911, possessed a great sense of humor and an almost Dickensian ability to describe a scene. In describing the troublemaker Jones, Phelps explained that Jones was "cussin' and swearin' in his room at a great rate the other day when somebody told him that the ventilator in the corner of the room at the top was a telephone connecting to the Admiral's office and that the Admiral could hear everything he said. He shut up immediately and next day he had the ventilator stuffed full of paper and a towel hung up over it. . . ."

Midshipman Phelps, who became Commodore Phelps, died as a result of an automobile accident on 23 December 1919.

US NAVAL ACADEMY OCTOBER 14TH 1877

My Dear Mother,

I received your letter and that book yesterday and I am so busy that I will not be able to write very much. I got a 3.3 in Trigonometry last week and a 3.59 on the exam. I have taken the elective course in Math and am studying Calculus which is as hard as can be. I am going to take the elective in Chemistry when they begin it which will be next term.

Last week a plebe named Conway signed his examination Cadet Plebe and when asked why he did so, he said that some upperclassmen told him to do so. He was reported for it and there will be an investigation about it. Then a court martial and then several bilging papers. I did not have anything to do with him or any other of them as I don't like 'em. There is one of them named Jones who was cussin' and swearin' in his room at a great rate the other day when somebody told him that the ventilator in the corner of the room at the top was a telephone connecting to the Admiral's office and that the Admiral could hear everything he said. He shut up immediately and next day he had the ventilator stuffed full of paper and a towel hung up over it and he was reported for having the towel hung up on the wall.

I stayed at the library all yesterday afternoon and I find that they have nearly every book that there is. I have been writing up a "skinny" (physics and chemistry) lecture all this afternoon and I will have to bone calculus as soon as I get through this letter.

I received a letter the other day telling me that one of the men who was on the cruise this summer had fallen from the top gallant yard of the Hartford and striking on deck was killed. We have to study Freeman's history this year and we have already gone over all that we went over last year. We had an exam last Friday and I think that I got a pretty good mark because I answered all the questions. I received a letter the other day from a fellow in New York named Sturmdorf, who knows Charley. He says he wants to get in and wants me to send him information. I never heard of him before and he don't know me but wrote because he knew Charley. I will send him one of those blue books in a few days. Tell Charley so if you see him soon. I will have to close now as space is getting small. Give my love to all the folks and write again soon to your loving son,

Harry

Harry Phelps *Courtesy USNA Nimitz Special Collections*

US NAVAL ACADEMY OCTOBER 22 1877

My Dear Mother,

I received your letter this morning. I suppose it laid in the post office over Tuesday as we do not receive any mail on that day. I looked for it all day Saturday and thought that it was very queer that it did not come. Tell Mr. Clark that I received his letter and will answer it as soon as I can get time to write what he wants me to. I don't think he wants a special answer right away. I got a 3.2 last week and a 2.71 on the exam last Thursday. It was an awful tough one and many low marks were knocked. I got a 2.7 on the History Exam. The subject of it was all the Freeman that we went over last year, the first term. I got a 2.4 on the same subject on the semi-annual last year.

Last Saturday we had a drill at the government farm. We captured the hospital again. This time we did not march over but went in boats and my division carried howitzers. We were told to put on working suits and old shoes in the morning and when we got to the farm we found out what for. We ran our boats, 14 of them, full of fellows, up on the beach behind a bluff, and as they would not go way up on land, we had to go in the water. I jumped way ashore and did not go in the water at all. The others, most of them, went in the water to carry the howitzers out of the boats. We fixed the howitzers and marched up nearly to the top of a hill and laid down until the order forward. Then we went up with a rush and a cheer and captured the hospital after a gallant resistance. We then marched back to the Academy and got there about 1 o clock. Whilst landing one of the buglers went to jump ashore and his foot slipped and he fell flat in the water. He asked the commanding officer to go home but was told to keep in the sun a little while and he would get dry.

I was swinging Indian Clubs the other day and in trying to get through a new motion when I cracked myself on the hip and raised quite a large bruise and I did it again the next day in the same place and my leg is quite stiff, but I suppose it will be all right in a day or two. I will have to close now as to get this in by taps as the mail goes then and you will probably get it Wednesday morning. Excuse writing on account of hurry. Give my love to all and write soon.

Your loving son,
Harry

US NAVAL ACADEMY OCTOBER 7 1877

My Dear Mother,

. . . We had a great storm here last Thursday. I guess it was the equinoctial. However, it was just like the one we had here on September 15, 1876. It blew down several trees. Among them was that large cherry tree by the bandstand and a beautiful willow behind the old building by the Armory. It is a curious fact that all the trees which were blown down that day were split. The trunks split from the crotch to the ground and one part fell on one side and the other fell on the other side. The immense tree on the drill ground was split but it did not fall down as the wind did not hold out long enough to blow it over. The water swamped two large sailing launches which were down by the Dale and also capsized Terry's catboat which was anchored there.

The only thing we cared about was our boat house which was blown down in the evening and we would not have cared so much if it had not been for the contents which consisted of 6 four-oared shells and 2 disc-oared shells and 3 single shells, all of which were mashed flat as pancakes and the next afternoon there was quite a crowd down there gathering shells and getting relics. I got a piece of 2 paper shells and of 1 cedar one. There were three cedar ones I think. They were the finest ones in the house. One belongs to our class. I suppose that another house will be built and the different classes will refurnish it with new shells. At present we have not got a single one. Our class had two which cost us $300 last year and now "Where Oh Where are they? Ask of the waves that silently roll over the graves of the shells now departed." Don't applaud.

Some of the boats had belonged in the Academy for over 10 years and were very highly prized by their owners in the several classes. . . . I will have to close now. Give my love to all the folks. Write soon and send that ring and oblige

Your Loving Son,
Harry

US NAVAL ACADEMY NOVEMBER 3 1877

My dear mother,

I received your letter this morning and as I am not very busy I will answer it tonight. I am very sorry that I got so many demerits last month and I am going to be as good as possible this month and not get many and will try to get some taken off before long. There is hardly an officer here that likes the proposed style of cap. One of them is on the board that is suggesting the uniform and the reason that he wants it is that he is bald on top of his head and a little way down behind and he wants a cap which he can put way back on his head and cover the bald spot and yet have it come down far enough in front to look well.

The other day I was exercising in the gymnasium and while vaulting over one of the horses I came down too heavy on my thumb and I guess I sprained it, however, it is swelled some and the doctor painted it and half of my hand with Iodine so that I look like an Indian. I suppose that it will be well in a day or two as I can use it a little now. The night before that I was trying something on the rings and when I dropped off I dropped too late and missed the cushion and rubbed up the floor with my face. I got up and thought I was hurt but on washing the dirt off I found that I was not even scratched. The canvas cover on the floor having kept me from being scratched.

This morning at seamanship drill the main topsail yard got jammed while lowering it and the halliards were taken off the pin and just then it got free and came down by the run and one of the lifts getting jammed it tilted way over to one side and the top gallant sternsail boom broke loose and came down on deck. It just missed a couple of fellows who were standing in the gangway and went into the very place that my roommate had vacated when he saw it coming down. I was aft by the mizzer rigging at the time and of course had to go to see if there was anybody hurt.

I got a 3.2 in math last week and a 3.0 on the exam. I don't expect to get much this month as I have a man who gives very low marks. I got a 2.8 in Skinny (Physics) last week. I will try to answer Mr. Clark's letter tomorrow if I get time. I am getting along well in everything and am going to try for a high number this year. The lessons are easy but we have so much outside work that all our time is taken up. We have to copy up note books, write skinny lectures every week and work a problem in descriptive. We will finish Freeman next Wednesday and I will not be a bit sorry. I will have to close now as it is nearly taps. Give my love to all and write soon to

Your Loving Son,
Harry

US NAVAL ACADEMY JANUARY 6 1878

My Dear Mother,

. . . There was a stag dance last night and I attended it and learned a good deal. These dances are those at which no one but Cadets are present and they afford a good opportunity for practice. I am learning to dance quite well now and can dance the Lancers, Waltz, and Polka. I want to practice as much as I can now so as to be able to dance well next summer when I come home and go to parties and picnics. I will be able to act a great swell and have a splendid time.

I went to a hop last Monday night and had a first rate time. The time seems to pass very quickly here and it does not seem to be more than a month since I left the Constellation and came back here. In two weeks the semi annual will be here and I will have lots of work before that time.

There is a man in the fourth class named Jones and he is about as hard a case as Jones was last year, if not a harder one. His last exploit was stealing two bags of powder from the Santee. He is confined on the Santee Saturdays and Sundays and holidays for Frenching and on New Years Day he took a piece of candle and lit it and went down into the magazine and picked up two bags (14 lbs) of powder and with them in one hand and the candle in the other, he came out again. He brought them up to the buildings and if he had not been "took" with them, there is no knowing what he would have done with them.

A second class engineer who fell down a hatch on the Mayflower on the Cruise of '76 two years ago died last week at his home. He was buried on Friday and the flags hung at half-mast for him. His name was Noell and he stood well in his class too.

On New Years Eve at 12 oclock 3 first class men went into the Yard and rang all the bells. The bell by the Admiral's house, the chapel bell,

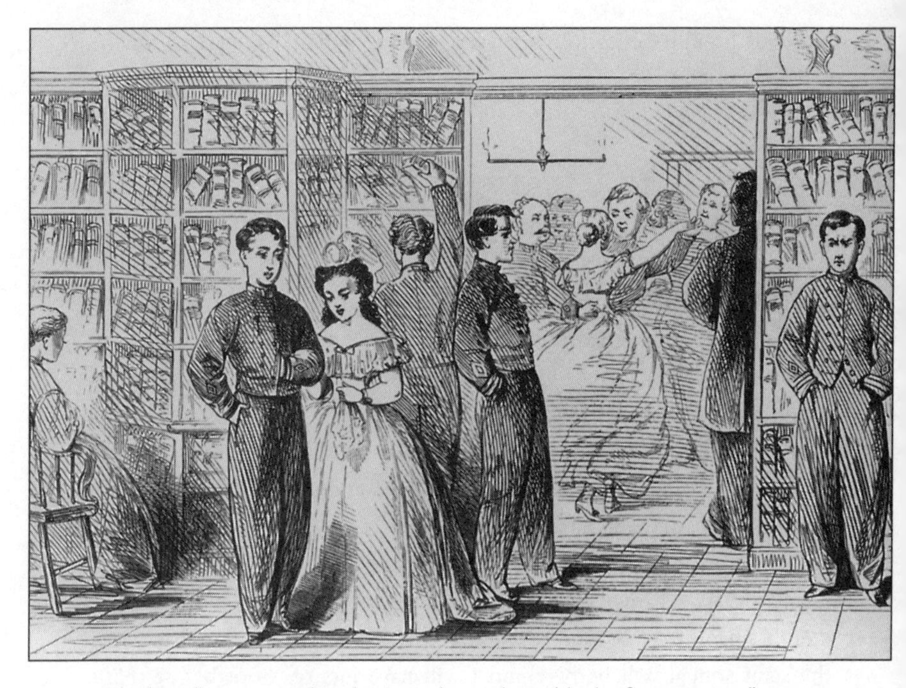

The hop: "I went to a hop last Monday night and had a first rate time." *Courtesy USNA Nimitz Library Archives*

the Jap bell, the working bell. In fact, every bell they could get at. For this they were all reduced and one man was a Cadet Master, one an Ensign and the other a Gun Captain.

We had a show yesterday afternoon by a "prestidigetateur" (I think that's right). He first explained a number of the tricks of celebrated magicians and then he showed us a number of tricks and some sleights of hand and juggling. He could manipulate things boss. He threw brass balls up and also knives, bottles, bells, and once he asked for two small men to come up on the stage to help him and two of the biggest men in the Academy went up.

The rest of the afternoon I spent in the library and part of the evening I bowled and I made the best score at three pins and what is called chinaman. The pins are set up like this [here Phelps drew an arch of dotted lines, with the letter "A" at one end of the arch] and in order to hit the pins the ball must be rolled in a curve around the dotted line as to hit the Chinaman (A) and we count one off for each time he was hit. I made a 42 which is the highest that has been made this year. I made 39 a while ago and another fellow made 41. I will have to close now as there is nothing more that I can think of to write about. You may suppose that as I write mostly about our sports I pay little attention to study but I only play on Saturdays and on holidays and I give the rest of my time to studying. We also play football sometimes and often a game gets very exciting. Give my love to all the folks. . . .

Your loving son,
Harry

US NAVAL ACADEMY JANUARY 28 1878

My Dear Mother,

I received your letter this morning and I will try to answer it now as tomorrow morning we have an exam and will be occupied until the afternoon as it begins at 8 and stops at 1. We had an exam in Trigonometry this morning and I did nearly all of them but will probably get about a 3.0 or there abouts. We have Constitution tomorrow and another exam in Trig Wednesday. Physics, Thursday. Descriptive, Friday. Calculus, Saturday. So you see that our time is pretty much all taken up and as each exam is 5 hours long it takes all the morning and the afternoon is occupied in studying for the next one.

My roommate spent all yesterday afternoon and evening writing gouges. He wrote 17 pages of foolscap on the matter in Trigonometry and he had not been in the examination room more than an hour when he was caught with them and will get a zero and will most likely be dropped as unsat. He only had to get a 1.2 and I told him last evening that he ought to study and not write gouge as he could easily get that much and he would run a chance of a zero if he got caught but he would not mind and so got "took."

There were several other ones "took" gouging this morning and as most of them are unsat, they will probably bilge.

I am alright so far as a zero in Math would not make me unsat and I have only to get a 1.5 in English and a 1.08 in Physics and I am pretty sure to make those marks.

Major General Schofield was down here from West Point last week and we had to drill for him and also today for some Rear Admiral who came down here. I don't think that we will have any more drills this week as I think we did not last year. It has rained here for two days but has let up today although it is quite windy and cloudy.

We had a problem to do in Descriptive on the semi-annual and we have to draw it first in our rooms and then hand it in and finally do it next Friday. There were three different problems and the Head of the Department picked out the best one of each kind from among the midshipmen and engineers. He picked out mine as the best one of the kind that I had and also two other midshipmen, one for each of the two other kinds and an engineer for each kind. We had to put ours in the best we knew how last Friday and we also were allowed to work on Saturday afternoon and Professor Hendrickson is going to have them bound in a big book of his. He has somebody do each problem and has them all bound and as our names are on them people who see the book can see our work. I feel as big as possible to think that he should pick mine out to bind and I have got good marks in it too.

I will send you my sketch which I handed in when I finish with it if I don't forget it and I will try not to, and you can see what sort of thing it is.

I was forgetting all together that my birthday was coming but since you speak of it I remember it. I am about 60½ inches high and weigh 7 stone. I am cultivating a moustache and sides and will look extremely bad when I come home with side wheels out. You can send me anything you wish for my birthday. I am not particular because there are so many things I could ask for that I could not decide on one so I will close for now. Give my love to all.

From Your loving Son,
Harry

US NAVAL ACADEMY MARCH 10 1878

My Dear Mother,

I received your letter yesterday morning and put it in my pocket until after drill and I was so busy that I did not think of it again until we were eating supper. Mr. Rose has not been to see me yet. I did not expect him. If you will send me his address I will write to him and find out how it goes with him. I got Matt's letter last Tuesday morning but as I had written Monday I did not write but a little letter to him. I wear collar size fifteen but you need not buy any new ones unless you want to. I only wanted a few old ones of Matt's or Frank's which they do not want to wear for Saturday evenings when I go to the hops. . . .

There is quite a budget of news from here this week. Friday afternoon a British boat came into the Roads in tow of a tug and the Captain came ashore and requested assistance from the Commandant as his crew had mutinied and would not work for him. An officer and eight Marines were sent on board of her and the crew of ten men and the 2nd mate and boatswain's mate were put in irons. She is still lying off here and waiting for another crew who will take her to her destination—Ireland—where the crew is to be tried for mutiny. They mutinied because they held that the ship was unseaworthy and they were afraid of her.

The other incident of importance was the foot ball match here. Fifteen of our class played with fifteen from St. John's College in Annapolis. It took some trouble to decide about the rules but they were all made before the game began. We had a large place laid off on the drill ground and bounded by a line of whitewash. The Admiral let us have a lot of flags to mark the goals and he also had two of the old buildings fixed up for some spectators. They started the game about three o clock and the first inning we won, the second they won, and we won the next three which was all they played as agreed before hand. So we finished them off this time. There is some talk of challenging them to play marbles or mumblepeg as they have been beaten every time that they have tried to play baseball or football with us. One could easily see after the first inning that they were no match for us as they were beginning to show signs of being tired out while our side were almost as fresh as when they began and were not even breathing fast. The way we get used to running is by having a good deal of double time mixed up in our drills so that we get good winds. Another way that we had the better of them was that we were allowed to shoulder them—that is to shove them over if they were too near the ball and I heard one of them say after the first inning, "My, how they do butt. One fellow caught me in the short ribs and doubled me right up" and I heard another one of them say that he had not been obliged to run so much for some time. These games of football are the most exciting things that I ever saw. . . . I can't help thinking about next summer but I am not going to let it keep me back at all but I hear that "half the pleasure is in the anticipation of it" and as I find it very pleasant I like to anticipate. When I come home I will paint all your fences, doors, windows and fix everything up slick and then will go in for a vacation. I see that my paper is getting small and so I will have to shut myself up. Give my love to all the folks.

Your loving Son,
Harry

US NAVAL ACADEMY APRIL 14 1878

. . . That midshipman Jones in the fourth class seems to be the biggest fool that ever was seen. Last Saturday he amused himself by going from the top of the house to the ground by means of a lightning rod. He also was reported for hanging out of the front windows several times. They had an exam yesterday and the paper which he handed in was something like this.

I. A zero on this would be agreeable to me.
II. This looks so difficult that I may not try it.
III. I don't know anything about this.
IV. I never "savied" progression.
V. Give it up.
VI. I don't know anything about signals. We get them when we get in the third class.
VII. I did not bone this subject.

You can imagine the mark he will receive on his papers. He was reported this morning for neglect of study for which he is reported nearly every day and for writing impertinent remarks on his examination paper. This is the one I told you about a long time ago. He stole powder from the Santee and was dismissed but got reinstated again by promising to reform and the way he reforms is at the rate of 8 reports a day. Nearly all of the men now here have come to the conclusion that he has not yet common sense.

While at Seamanship drill yesterday a second classman got his left hand jammed and he will have to have a couple of joints of his fingers taken off if he does not lose his whole hand. He stood very high last year and had single diamond and would in all probability have had some stripes next year. Now he will probably lose so much time recovering that he will not know very much at the annual which is now fast approaching and won't stand so high. . . . I will have to close now as my time is limited. Give my love to all the folks. There are only 67 days more.

Your loving Son,
Harry

US NAVAL ACADEMY OCTOBER 22 1878

My Dear Mother,

I received your card yesterday but was unable to sit up long enough to answer it so I had to put it off until today. I was taken with one of my sick headaches on Sunday and am still on the sick list with it and confined to my bed. I thought you would be looking for a letter so I attempted to write one this morning. I do not think I can make much of a success of it as my head is jumping around as if dissatisfied with its quarters and wanted to change them. I intend to turn in as soon as I finish this.

Last Saturday night I went to a hop at the gymnasium and was introduced to several young ladies and danced with them all. I did not intend to go but after supper I met one of the fellows who asked me if I was going and when I said no, he said that he had somebody to whom he wished to introduce me so I had to fix up real fine and go and the pleasure fully repaid me for the trouble I took in getting ready. Besides the lady I spoke of invited me to call upon her in the city of Annapolis where she lives and of course I will have to go and so I will have some place to which I can go when I have liberty on Saturday afternoons instead of roaming around the city in an aimless manner.

Sunday afternoon I went walking in the Yard with one of the fellows and met two of the ladies I knew, walking in the yard and if I had been alone I should have embraced the opportunity—but I let it pass and the saying is "opportunity has hair in front but bald behind and if you catch her by the forelock you have her, but once let her pass and Jupiter himself could not overtake her." The chance is gone.

It is too bad that you are not going away. That is for you. Of course, it is all the better for me as I shall be able to hear from you oftener and possibly to see you down here before the season or rather year is over and you ought to come down for you have nothing to do for any great length of time and could easily spare a week or so down here and the trip would do you good too. I shall expect to see you before a very long time and you must not say no.

Everything is quiet here as far as the outside world but I am not in a condition that can be called quiet. So you must excuse my writing as I have to look at it sidewise being unable to hold my head up any longer. I will try to finish this sheet though before I stop and would like to get an answer by Saturday. . . .

Your loving son,
Harry

US NAVAL ACADEMY OCTOBER 19 1879

My dearest Mother,

Matt's letter excusing you from writing was received yesterday but hereafter no such excuses will be accepted, excepting in cases of urgent necessity and then I suppose they will have to be whether I want to or not.

There is nothing of much account going on here—merely the same routine day after day. Studies, recitation, exercises, and recreation follow one another with a monotony that is very displeasing to a person after having spent a short time in more agreeable pursuits at home. We are having the same melting weather right along. Today we had a heavy rain squall and the wind veered to the northwest so that it is now somewhat cooler.

. . . We had considerable excitement down here on Friday evening caused by a fight between a couple of midshipmen. The row began before supper and after supper the 1st classmen stood on the stairways and in the corridor by the mess hall door to mob one of the parties who declared he would not fight (he having given the provocation) and the officer in charge saw that something was up but he could not tell what and so was in a terrible stew. He had watchmen all over the new building and a lot of marines and sent every first classmen out.

The interested parties, however, came down to quarters and before the authorities knew anything about it, the thing was all over. It wound up by one of the pugilists tripping and falling against the edge of a door, thereby cutting in his head a gash about 4 inches long. The fall knocked what little sense he had left out of him and we laid him out on a bed and got one of the doctors. We brought him to and did what we could until the doctor arrived when he fixed up his cuts and bruises and placed his name on the sick list. Both parties are now in the hospital. The commandant heard about it and came down to our building to find how government property (midshipmen) had been damaged and had quite a time. I expect there will be more disturbance when the parties recover. . . . Write soon. Love to all from your loving son,

Harry

NAVAL ACADEMY JANUARY 27 1880

My dear Mother,

We are right in the midst of our semi-annual examination just now but I don't have another one until Thursday so I can easily take time to write a letter. Yours came very opportunely this morning. Received it just after returning from our examination in Shipbuilding. I wrote 32 pages of foolscap on the subject and then could only say about ¾ of what I wished to. I had to be short so that I would not find the time up when I had not yet finished. We were examined in gunnery yesterday and I wrote 23 pages on the subject. Thursday morning we have our exam in Navigation which is my strong point. I am trying hard to stand 1st in it for the term but am doubtful as to my success thus far. . . .

Last Saturday evening the Ladies gave a large Leap Year Party in the gymnasium which was a decidedly successful affair. My sweetheart escorted me to it and saw we were well provided for during the evening and I don't think I ever enjoyed myself so much before. I suppose you know the rules and regulations of these parties.

The festivities ended at eleven o clock and then I escorted my young lady home. It is about the time of full moon now and I am rather spooney so you can easily judge what sort of time we had on the way out. I had liberty until 11:40 and did not get out there until 11:30 and I stayed for fully ten minutes and then had to make tracks to get in at the proper time. I managed to do it though.

The next day after breakfast and before church we had a miniature fox hunt using a mouse for a fox. One of the fellows caught a mouse in a large trap and about ten of us armed ourselves with brooms, bats, snow shovels, lacrosse sticks, and swords and took the ferocious monster out in the center of the parade ground. Then he was let go and such a chase we had. In the course of the pursuit I got within striking distance of the animal and of course made a desperate stroke at it whereto my sword snapped off right in the middle of the blade and I was without means of defence having only the handle and a small portion of the blade left in my hand. . . .

I expect my chances for graduation are pretty good now so I have been measured for my outfit. Have already tried on my service and full dress uniforms and they fit first rate. This tailor in town is the best one I ever knew. He can make better clothes and better fits for moderate prices than any other tailor I know of. What do you think of having to buy two coats at $40 each? One service and one full dress. I tell you it takes the cash to graduate from this 'yer mansion but Uncle Sam is good for it all. After my name on the paymaster's roll appears a sum sufficient to cover all my expenses at the end of the year.

After I graduate I am going to spend a few days in Washington and then I am going home with Van Druzler to Elvira to stay a short space. I may stay a week or so in Annapolis for all I know now it seems to have more attractions than it used to have—for me at least.

I can remember the time when my one idea was to get out of this town but my how things have changed, since at times I really feel sorry that the end is so near and there again when something occurs to forcibly remind me of the restraint under which I am placed, the old longing returns with all its force and I make resolutions to study hard so that the time will seem, at least, to pass more rapidly, but when the time comes to study I find myself unable to study anymore than I otherwise would had I made no resolve.

Why don't you take a day or two and run down here. It does not cost so very much and the trip I know would do you ever so much good. A very good time to come down would be next week. Get here Saturday morning, the 7th of February and stay until Monday morning. Do not make excuses, now, but come right along. You may as well enjoy yourself while you have a chance and it will give me great pleasure to have you come down. You have not been here for nearly three years now and you don't know how things have changed. Next time you write I don't want to hear anything but that you are coming down.

I am glad to hear that Hattie is getting along so well and hope she will continue to do so. I wrote to her some time ago. I guess she will answer when she feels exactly like it. By the way it just occurred to me Hattie's middle name is Lizzie and I am going to call her by it. I think it is very nice. My sweetheart's name is Lizzie, whence the preference. I suppose you are getting about sick of hearing me write of nothing but of my sweetheart but I suppose you know how it is under the circumstances. I'm gone. . . . Hoping for a letter soon and to see you soon too, I remain,

Your loving son,
Harry

CHAPTER 6

The Newspapers Are Exaggerating

The Letters of Alfred K. Schanze

A decided advantage of midshipman life is the chance to participate in national events. A perennial disadvantage is the necessity of enduring public scrutiny. During his academy career, Alfred Schanze, a native of New Jersey and a member of the class of 1908, experienced both.

He was a USNA student when Midshipman James R. Branch, class of 1907, died from injuries suffered in a fight with Minor Merriweather Jr., class of 1908. The fight, a fairly routine midshipman activity, took place in Bancroft Hall. Not until the next morning did the severity of the event become clear. Having slipped into a coma, Branch did not awaken. Taken to a hospital, Branch did not recover from the coma and died. The ensuing Branch–Merriweather scandal stunned the nation. Shortly after the furor abated, a hazing scandal erupted at the academy, which once again sparked national indignation. Schanze, while fully aware of the seriousness of both the Branch–Merriweather tragedy and the hazing inquiry, also knew "as usual the newspapers are greatly exaggerating all that takes place at the Academy."

In 1906 the academy garnered national attention of an entirely different nature as the body of John Paul Jones came to Annapolis. Schanze was also impressed: "After the speeching we followed J.P.J. up to quarters to the tune of the funeral march and stood there about twenty minutes while the casket was being jacked into place in the lobby. . . . The whole ceremony was about the most impressive I have ever witnessed and I shall remember it for years to come."

Having served his country faithfully in World War I, Schanze remained vitally interested in the academy and the navy until his death in 1950.

Alfred K. Schanze *Courtesy* The Lucky Bag/*USNA Nimitz Special Collections*

JULY 6 1904

Dear Papa,

I am now a midshipman in a sailor suit. My suit case is being expressed to you at Jersey City and the key is herewith enclosed. My deposit amounted to $255 and I wrote up the entire amount on one check, so I am herewith returning the other check, also my pass. My room is all settled now and I begin work tomorrow.

The weather here is very hot but our suits are more comfortable than citizens clothes.

Remember me to everybody at home.

Very sincerely,

Alfred K.

JULY 7, 1904

Dear Mamma,

I am fast getting used to the routine here and will be able to write you a little better when I get used to my hours. Today we have nothing but drills. The only clothes I have at present are white and working suits and I feel very sloppy in these. My white service uniforms will not be ready for at least ten days.

The weather has been very hot and sultry and we all have been made uncomfortable by it. Just received a letter from Mr. Hayward extending me his congratulations.

Please remember me to everyone.

I remain sincerely,
Alfred K.

JULY 9 1904

Dear Mamma

Received your letter yesterday and was very glad to hear from you, but sorry that you are having bad weather. I have settled down to hard steady work and am always tired when evening comes. At 6:00 a. m. we get up and at 6:30 breakfast begins after the formation. From 7:20 until 8:00 we must sweep our rooms and make our beds. After this drills begin. Yesterday we all rowed in the cutters until our hands were sore and backs lame. This, however, is a very invigorating training and when I am all done I expect to be about six times as strong as before entering.

12:15 P.M.

I began this letter at 7:30 a.m. but as the bugle called us to our work I had to quit. We had another cutter drill and got more blisters. When you want to come down and see me just let me know. Come of a Saturday and stay over Sunday and I will be able to come out to see you on each of those days in the afternoon. The best place for you to stay is Carvel Hall. I have not yet received my white service uniform so I shall have to stay here today and possibly tomorrow also, but I do not mind that as I have lots of letters to write. There are still some new fellows coming every day and they, you see, are even greener than I am. Lots of these chaps are homesick and very much disappointed with the work here but I like it more every day.

Remember me to all at home and also to Mabel.

With love from
Alfred K.

DECEMBER 29, 1904

My dear Papa,

A jag is a dangerous playtoy almost everywhere but here at USNA it becomes positively fatal to sport one about. Those unlucky fellows who are now aboard our "houseboat" were not by any means the only chaps who had intoxicating drinks here on Christmas. When I left you on Saturday night and came in here I met at least a dozen midshipmen who were listing to starboard and to port like a ship with a hole in the bottom. This cannot be helped, as there are black sheep in every fold. You need not give me a single thought in this respect as I am perfectly well able to control myself. My companions are all of my own selection and they imitate me, not I them.

I hardly think anyone will be dismissed or that any were even recommended for dismissal. All, however, have been given one hundred demerits, sent to the ship for the rest of the year and deprived of September leave. This in itself is a heavy punishment although the Supt. issued an order on the subject in which he called it "this comparatively light punishment." The Supt. deals as fairly with all of us and although I belong to a small minority who think the Supt. right, I shall maintain my stand against all comers. . . .

Hoping you are all well

I remain sincerely,
Alfred K.

MARCH 5 1905

My Dear Papa

. . . I suppose you have read all about the inauguration by now and know more about it than I do, as I have read but little about the show, and save only my small part of the performance. We fellows tried our level best to look well although hampered by overcoats. The wind was something ferocious to face. It kept lifting our hats off and drove the street dust into our faces with stinging force. During the President's address we stood at parade rest directly before his stand at the Capitol. We were face to the wind which at times actually made the whole ranks stagger and wave like branches. After the address the President drove to the White House for a short luncheon before the review. The parade with the West Point Cadets in the lead followed in the wake of the Presidential barouche but was halted during the luncheon of the presidential party. This halt lasted forty-five minutes. My company was immediately in front of the Southern Railway Building where the wind had a good chance at us owing to the openness of the street at that point. When we passed the reviewing stand before the White House our line was absolutely perfect and we were cheered in a way which ought to have given us very big opinions of ourselves. If we had been allowed to remain in Washington to attend the Ball as the West Pointers did I believe we should have developed "swelled" heads. I am sorry you and Mamma were not there to see it all.

In my lessons I have been doing as always. My marks for last month you must have by now. I am not overworking a bit but manage to stay among the first third of the class. What are the chances of a war in 1908 or 1909? I think there ought to be one scheduled for about that time. If it comes I shall be right in line to do what Dewey did if I do not do what Bagaley did first. The Japs and those half breed Tartars called Russians seem to be shooting a good deal of chilled steel at each other again. The Japs do not seem to need me to show them how to do their part of the business. The licking they are giving the Russians suits me to a finish. I have not had anything tickle me so much since Arminius kicked Varus out of the German woods in 110 A.D.

With love
I remain
Alfred K.

MARCH 5, 1905

My dear Mamma,

The inauguration has come and gone but I am just the same as ever in spite of the strenuous march we had. Our brigade most certainly was at its best as you may know by what the papers have to say about us. I do wish you could have been down at the capitol to see the parade. I do not believe there has been one as good since the Grand Army parade of 1865. We chaps worked hard and tried our level best and I am of the opinion that we met with success. You should have heard the cheers we received during the entire march. Navy! Navy! Navy! sounded from every stand and every street crowd we passed. It was enough to give us all a heap of conceit but everyone is normal. . . .

With love to all
I remain sincerely,
Alfred K.

MAY 3 1905

My dear Mamma,

Your letter reached me this morning and I was glad to read about your scheme for Papa's birthday. I shall probably send you one of my cards. In fact I shall enclose one with this letter, but I should like to get Dad a little something and send it from here as I know he will appreciate my thinking of him myself, even though what I send him may not cut much ice.

Yesterday was a day of unusual activity with us. We, the brigade, turned out in full dress . . . to act as a funeral escort up to the West Street Station. This is rather a strenuous job in warm weather as we have to keep very slow step and properly braced up so as to look respectable. We did not get back until twelve o' clock.

In the afternoon we had a sham battle. Every midshipman was equipped with forty rounds of blank cartridges. We marched out upon the broad lawn which surrounds Lover's Lane and began war in earnest. We did real shooting, real charging with the bayonet, but only sham dying. I was ordered to die early in the game, which order I carried out very promptly as it was very easy to lie perfectly still upon my stomach. The battle field looked very realistic with its numerous dead lying scattered all over, but it must have looked funny to see all of us corpses jump up and run like blazes when the bugle sounded the assembly. You will see all this repeated during June Week and you will know what it all means. Do not get frightened when you see a chap running along for all he is worth and then suddenly fall upon his face, for he has received orders to become a corpse at his earliest convenience, and is probably trying to make it look as realistic as possible. . . .

I hope you are well and having such fine weather as we are here. Give my love to the children, to Dad and to Aunt Annie, and keep some yourself.

Sincerely,
Alfred K.

NOVEMBER 19 1905

My dear Papa

. . . We had a novel interesting mimic war yesterday morning which I shall tell you about. The First Battalion, consisting of companies one through six, and the Second Battalion, consisting of companies seven through twelve were opposing forces. The two battalions, each went half as artillery and half as infantry. A start of twenty minutes was given the First Battalion to go off among the fields and hills and take up a defensive position. It was the job of the Second Battalion whose commander knew nothing beforehand of his enemy's movements to follow and dislodge us of the First.

Well, the First marched on the double to a point just across the A.W.B. Railroad and there got ready for the attack. We cut armfuls of brush and made a long cover of about one hundred yards, on the brow of a hill. The three companies of infantry of which mine was one lay down behind this cover. The artillery selected several little risings of ground and also built masks.

For half an hour there was no sign of the searchers so our Commander, Lt. Commander Reed wrote some false orders and gave them to a scout with orders to let himself be captured. The trick worked very well and the enemy walked most beautifully into the trap. When we had them just where we wanted them we opened fire with blank cartridges and theoretically annihilated them. Of course, they ran away and took up positions of defense upon the various hills. We kept up a running fight all the way back to Academy grounds.

This whole thing was a new experience for us and a little hard on our skin, as the fields in this neighborhood are uncultivated and are just covered with wild roses. My knees are all frayed out from rose thorn scratches. While we were firing from our breastworks, a much scared rabbit broke cover on the left flank and ran the full length of our defense firing line within fifteen feet of our rifles. He surely was in a hurry as he made about forty knots.

I received the box of chicken in perfect condition last night and was agreeably surprised by it. Bubbles and I will enjoy that grub all day as it is cold, dreary and rainy here for a change. Will send you football tickets within two days.

Very affectionately
Alfred K.

DECEMBER 16 1905

My dear Papa,

Your letter enclosing clippings from the N.Y. Sun reached me and were very interesting. The Court Martial is now over and Merriweather got out of the deal. When his letter from the Secretary was read out before the Brigade, I really felt very sorry for him as Bonaparte wrote him a very strong letter, which was probably as rough on him as any of the previous experience.

With regard to the hazing there is much to be said on both sides. To begin with the Superintendent has authorized a most underhanded investigation. I do not want to give you the impression that I am in the least worried about the matter as far as I myself am concerned because all the investigations Sands makes will never bother me; but I do consider the behavior of some of my class mates as pretty serious for them.

The investigating board is proceeding somewhat after this manner; they bring up a "plebe" and then take the muster list of his company and start with the First Class, asking him, "Has this man ever hazed you?" This method was adopted before the Kimborough case occurred and really led to the latter affair. Mr. Kimborough of the Fourth Class apparently is of a pretty low order and the first thing he did when he came up before the Commandant was squeal. That of course got every upperclassman in the place down upon him and they swore they would bilge the rascal. While he may have been a little severely treated by Coffin, he, nevertheless, was by no means brutally handled and was not really unconscious. His behavior was nothing more or less than another squeal and has caused all the subsequent measures on the part of the authorities here.

As usual the newspapers are greatly exaggerating all that takes place at the Academy and seem to take special delight in giving the national institution as bad a name as they can. My advice to you is not to say much or believe much of what you see even in the N.Y. Sun. I shall keep you informed of the proceedings here and my information is absolutely correct. I cannot understand that spirit in the American people that will allow such a fellow as the editor of the Boston Globe to call the midshipmen a crowd of hoodlums and ruffians. If he ever shows his face inside of Academic limits, he will probably be strongly convinced that his statement is true.

That so called standing on the head is not exactly what most people think. The fellow who does the stunt puts his head and hands upon the floor and then jumps his feet about three inches from the floor. It is of course a pretty violent form of exercise and something which the YMCA attempted to stop, with but little success. It looks as if almost all the upperclassmen who have put the plebes on their heads will get some serious punishment and I am afraid Bubbles will come in for his share as he has done far more hazing than a fellow of good judgement ought to do. Add to this fact that his mark in Math is 2.23 and you can see that his name will be mud when he goes before the Board. I rather believe that he is very slow to see consequences in the future and all kinds of talk cannot make him use good sense.

The weather is fierce; Yesterday it snowed all day. Last night it froze, and this morning it is raining.

Give my love to Mamma and the children.

Very sincerely yours,

Alfred K.

JANUARY 17 1906

My dear Papa,

From the present method of procedure it looks as though the hazing inquests were going to last indefinitely. Today at dinner formation the dismissals of two First Classmen and one Third Classman were announced. There are at present two more midshipmen on trial and Bloebaum is under arrest awaiting his trial which will probably start tomorrow. By being under arrest I do not mean to convey the idea that he is confined; he is simply suspended from all duty, recitations, and drills. There are six charges against him at present and he thinks that many more will be made before he is through. In a conversation he had last evening with Lieutenant Commander Robinson, Bubbles was informed that he was absolutely sure of bilging in Mathematics, which circumstance will make his chances before the Court Martial very small. Add to this the fact that he is unsatisfactory for the term in conduct and the result will be Good Bye Bubbles. We are all very sorry for him, but cannot in any way help him out of this scrape of his own making.

From the various bits of gossip that have been floating around lately it appears that the Superintendent is determined to get rid of all hazers. When a midshipman receives his specifications, as Bloebaum did yesterday, his doom is practically sealed, and the Court Martial is a matter of form.

It is an unfortunate thing for two First Classmen to be thrown out within a month of the day of their graduation, but it simply goes to show how determined the authorities are to punish all offenders. I am of the opinion that we may lose as many as a hundred midshipmen as a result of these proceedings. . . .

Very sincerely

Your son,

Alfred K.

APRIL 23 1906

My dear Mamma

Tomorrow I shall be at ceremonies almost all day, so I shall write your birthday letter this evening. First of all I wish you many happy returns of the day. On Wednesday I shall think of you all day and wish I could be home to help you celebrate but as I cannot come, you will have to trink eine tasse for me and have a slice of the regulation zimmet kuchen. When I receive your cake from Days I shall have a little celebration of my own. I wish to thank you for my dollar which got here in your letter this morning and also for the one I received in your letter last Wednesday shortly after I mailed you my letter.

Today we had a real true disturbance here in town which made quite a commotion and some lively moving on the part of the midshipmen. At quarter before six this morning, just when we all were soundest asleep, the siren sounded the fire signal. It did not take us more than three minutes to get up, dress slightly and run to our stations. Heavy clouds of black smoke came with the high wind from the direction of Sick Quarters and, of course, the first impression was that that building was burning. The hose reel squads, hook and ladder squads and bucket brigades at once went for their implements, while my company, which has no specific duty assigned, ran for the fire at top speed. When we got to the walk between the Officers Club and the hospital we saw the laundry was ablaze from end to end. Our hoses were rapidly in firing condition but it became evident at once that the laundry was beyond hope, and as the flames and sparks were landing thickly on the roofs of the Club and the hospital we turned the water on those buildings and got them thoroughly wet so that they were safe from the effect of heat and sparks. From then on we were busy with the fire itself. All the hoses we had we turned right into the windows from four sides at once. Most of us forgot what little damage there might be and poked the brass nozzles right into the doors and windows. To save the laundry was out of the question, and our efforts were directed merely toward extinguishing the flames.

By six forty five the fire had ceased to be dangerous and the midshipmen were relieved by sailors and marines. It was then that we had an op-

An alarm fire at the Naval Academy. "The hose reel squads, hook and ladder squads and bucket brigades at once went for their implements." *Courtesy USNA Nimitz Library Archives*

portunity to look each other over. When I turned out, I took off my pajamas and put on shoes, working pants and a heavy jersey and a watch cap. Lots of the fellows had slipped heavy jerseys over their pajamas and put on gym shoes. With the four hoses or more going on all sides we all got thoroughly soaked, and to add to the misery all the newly turned ground became mud, which, of course, climbed all over us. The whole crowd was a wet, muddy looking bunch and we all ran to quarters promptly and got thoroughly washed. At seven fifteen we had breakfast and at seven fifty we started for our first recitation as if nothing unusual had happened. This afternoon we drilled for nearly two hours, rehearsing the stunts for tomorrow, and tomorrow the fun will last about five hours, during most of which time we shall be on our feet.

The destruction of the laundry leaves us somewhat stranded for the present at least, as the new laundry is not quite ready for use. Besides the loss of machinery which will amount to a round sum when figured up, we lost about four hundred dollars worth of the table linen yesterday. There are forty tables in use in our mess hall and the linen is renewed every day. You can see how much we lost.

I shall make mental notes of all that takes place tomorrow and write Papa a complete description of all the doings. . . .

Again wishing you a very happy birthday,

I remain with love
Alfred K.

APRIL 27 1906

My dear Father,

I want to tell you a few things about the John Paul Jones ceremonies as I saw them on Tuesday. In the morning we had only two hours of study and recitations, and at ten fifteen we formed as for church formation, only in service uniform. We then marched over to the Armory and were dismissed until the early dinner formation. After dinner we had a little time to spare before the one fifteen full dress formation.

During the morning large numbers of people flocked in from all sides, and Annapolis was more crowded than I have ever seen it before.

All the ships out off the harbor mouth began to send in their details of sailors and marines and officers by the score. The French were all fixed up for the occasion and there was all kind of excitement and hurry. At least eighteen yachts of various kinds were anchoring all around the sea walls and then the lighter cruisers, three in all, came sailing in from beyond the light house and added their commotion to the already busy harbor. Large excursion steamers crowded with people came down from Baltimore. While special trains brought crowds from Washington.

At one fifteen we formed again in front of quarters and then the real fun was on. The Second Battalion marched over to the Armory and drew up on the side toward the city. Our first battalion marched over to the Superintendent's house to act as escort for the President. We stood for twenty minutes at parade rest while all the lesser lights came out of the house, and then for some reason or other, we were brought to attention for another twenty minutes before the President showed up. The line of march was then taken up, out through the Oklahoma gate, down King George Street and into the main gate at Maryland Avenue. A couple of troops of the regular cavalry who are stationed across the River at our rifle range for practice were drawn up throughout the line of march. There were horsemen on both sides of the street facing each other, at intervals of about ten feet, right up to Maryland Avenue gate.

When we entered the gate, we found the French drawn up on both curbs, and stretching all the way down to the main walk that leads to the Armory. This walk, Blake Row, was manned by American seamen and a finer sight will rarely be seen than those white hatted, blue jackets with their brown leggings and still browner faces. All along the route there were, I should safely say, thousands of people. All of the grass plot between Lover's Lane and Blake Row, from Maryland Avenue to Bancroft Hall, the terraces and even that high wall around the Superintendents new house were simply packed with sight seers.

As we approached the Armory our Battalion took up double time and drew up on the south side to let the President enter by the small door on that side. We then followed the Second Battalion in through the main door.

The John Paul Jones ceremony, 1906. "After the speeching we followed J.P.J. up to quarters to the tune of the funeral march and stood there for about twenty minutes while the casket was being jacked into place in the lobby." *Courtesy USNA Nimitz Library Archives*

I wish you could have seen that Armory. Every square foot of floor space was occupied by chairs. We midshipmen were placed on double rows of benches along the sides and when we sat down you could hardly notice us. On Monday I was in the Armory and counted four thousand chairs on the floor. It looked like even more people than that when all the people were seated and the gallery was stacked all the way around, four deep. At the far end of the building there was a high stand with tier on tier of seats. On this the Oratorio Society of Baltimore stood singing the Star Spangled Banner just as we entered. As nearly as I could see there were between two hundred and two hundred and seventy five singers in that bunch and the music they made was great to hear.

I shall not attempt to tell you anything about what each speaker said, but with Secretary Bonaparte acting as introducer they are in order: President Roosevelt, the French Ambassador, General Porter and Governor Warfield.

After the speeching we followed J.P.J. up to quarters to the tune of the funeral march and stood there about twenty minutes while the casket was being jacked into place in the lobby. After that ceremony we hustled the President back to the Superintendent's house and made for the quarters as fast as we could. We did not return to the Armory to put up the guns but were dismissed in front of Bancroft Hall. When I got to my room it was just six fifteen. The whole ceremony was about the most impressive I have ever witnessed and I shall remember it for years to come.

This month has but one more week and then will come the last pull of the academic year. I expect to have fair marks this month but nothing extra, as the spring fever has crept into my constitution and bylaws.

Give my love to Mamma and the children.

Affectionately, your son,
Alfred K.

CHAPTER 7

I Play My Violin

The Letters of Ellsworth Davis

The city of Annapolis did not impress Ellsworth Davis when he arrived at the academy in 1909. To his mother, he bemoaned the dullness of the town: "This is the deadest place I was ever in and there is absolutely nothing of interest to write about. The natives here and people who have lived here long enough to get the habit, walk along the streets at the rate of about a mile a week."

While his letters offer compelling details about the funeral of Fighting Bob Evans and the inauguration of President Wilson, Davis's correspondence also reveals his love of music. He mentioned a fellow named Butler: "He has a flute and we have played together once." In December 1909, Davis announced that "after much deliberation I bought a banjo." The 1911 prohibition against whistling in the corridors imposed severe limitations on this midshipman who loved to fill the air with tunes of any sort.

When he was not writing home to Connecticut about musical matters, Davis, who graduated in 1913, reported on other interesting Yard events. "There was quite an excitement Monday," he told his mother on 27 April 1910. "A lieutenant, who owns an automobile, was driving around the yard with a woman. She was managing the wheel. They came around the gym pretty fast and almost struck a telegraph pole. She dodged the pole very neatly but then turned the wrong way and shot right off the sea wall into about ten feet of water." Davis explained that both woman and officer got out alive but "a poor little dog, chained to the car, had to stay below and drown."

A career naval officer with a lifelong love of music, Cdr. Ellsworth Davis died on 18 January 1946.

31 MARYLAND AVENUE ANNAPOLIS MD
APRIL 28 1909 10:15 P.M.

Dear Mother,

It is awfully nice to get letters from home so often. This is a little farther off than I like to be. This is the deadest place I was ever in and there is absolutely nothing of interest to write about. The natives here and people who have lived here long enough to get the habit, walk along the streets at the rate of about a mile a week. Everything else corresponds. If you go into a store, you are very apt to find the storekeeper fast asleep. If you wake him and he finds that you are not quite sure what you want, instead of trying to sell you something, he lets you look over the stock and tells you to put the money in his pocket when you take something but not to disturb him again. . . .

This week I studied 11 hours Sunday; 11 hours Monday; 11 hours 45 minutes Tuesday; and 10½ hours today. I won't get through all the work but I am learning a lot of useful information which I would never have learned at home. Taps were blown about ¼ of an hour ago so I think that I must stop here. Sending lots of love to all.

Your devoted son,
Ellsworth

US NAVAL ACADEMY ANNAPOLIS MD JULY 3 1909

Dear Father,

In our book of regulations it is stated that all midshipman are "Mr." It does not call them naval officers however. Tell anyone that I am very much delighted for his or her felicitations and congratulations. . . . We rise at 6:30 and keep on the jump all day. There is "formation" before everything we do. An old bell rings and we all beat it down to the rotunda. There we line up, are inspected, i.e. to see whether we wear our clothes properly, have our shoes blacked, etc. Then we "count off" and march to the dining hall. There are a few minutes right after breakfast, then another "formation" and we all march over to the armory and drill. After a while we march back and go to boat drill. I was the starboard stroke oar in our boat this morning and the old sailor in charge told me

Ellsworth Davis *Courtesy* The Lucky Bag */ USNA Nimitz Special Collections*

that I had pulled an oar before. There are several more drills. Then dinner formation. Yesterday afternoon we went to Marine Engineering. Then we went down to the swimming tank. Everyone has to try to qualify i.e. he has to swim for five minutes. If he is unable to do this he must stay in the tank this summer until he learns to swim. If he qualifies he goes out in the river. Thursday evening we went to recreation hall where some of the boys are made to stand on their heads and sing solos. Last night we went to the gym. The gym is very fine. I almost croaked before bed-time. It will be all right after I get used to it i.e. if I don't kick the bucket while getting used to it. The bugle is just getting ready to blow supper and we have this p.m. off. Further particulars will follow.

Affectionately,
Ellsworth

US NAVAL ACADEMY ANNAPOLIS MD JULY 3 1909

Dear Mother,

Since I wrote you yesterday morning a great deal has gone on. It seems a great deal more than two days ago that I entered this place. After I wrote yesterday, we drilled in the armory and then we boys who just entered the day before went to the store to get the remainder of our outfits. In the afternoon, we had marine engineering and naval construction. Then we went to the gymnasium and had a swimming test. The test was to swim for five minutes. If found qualified the fellows can go swimming in the river. If not they must go in the tank and learn. I qualified. Last night we went to the gym. We exercised all around and then ran around the track. I was ready for bed all right when the time came. This morning, after breakfast, we drilled in the armory with muskets and then we all went out on the ship and climbed masts. Then we had boat drill. There is nothing going on here except the daily routine and I am afraid this is not very interesting for any one to read. It is now Saturday afternoon and we have a rest. It is against the rules for us to sit or lie on our beds between morning call and 9:30 P.M. except Saturday and Sunday after dinner. There is a great breeze blowing in my window today. My roommate is a boy named Keisker who comes from Louisville Ky. I should be very much obliged if you would send me some postage stamps. You know that you suggested it and I could use some to advantage. I wish that I were in Hampton. Love to all.

Affectionately,
Ellsworth

US NAVAL ACADEMY ANNAPOLIS MD JULY 9 1909

Dear Mother,

Got vaccinated. Every fellow has to do that and my turn came last night with about twenty others. Consequently, I get out of swimming for about ten days, I guess. I was intending to set to work and become a fairly strong swimmer but I have been there only once and now can't go at all so I haven't accomplished much as yet. The other boys are swimming and the vax ones have recreation time. I don't get very tired so don't worry any about that.

We always have beans Thursday night and bean soup Friday, also blackberry pie on Fridays. Please let me know if I write too often. Never having been away from home very long before, I don't know how often to write.

We had a fire drill this afternoon. It was quite extensive and the most strenuous thing of the kind I ever saw. We had to get out hook and ladder wagons and hose wagons. There are four companies. The one I am in, that is the third, had to run to a hydrant with a hose, hitch it up and the appointed nozzle men played the water on an imaginary fire. Another company or two had a big hook and ladder wagon and they raised ladders against the sides of the engineering building. I managed to qualify on the 300 yards range kneeling yesterday. The boys who qualify on all the rifles go over to the rifle range across the river and shoot. I believe that there is a rifle team too. I got a letter from Miss Harriett Robbins this morning which began "My dear niece Ellsworth." She congratulated me on straightening out my big toe. My roommate just returned from swimming. He said the water was great. Do the fellows go much in Hampton? We were going to build a dam in the brook and make a fine swimming hole but I got stuck here. Did the others do it?

Affectionately,
Ellsworth

ANNAPOLIS MD JULY 11 1909

Dear Father,

My roommate's name is Keisker. It is funny that you couldn't make it out for the fellow who calls the roll of the company at formation gets it different every time. It is anything from Hasker to Whisker. His grandmother was German but his father and mother have always lived in Louisville.

Spelling and Grammar come under English. In regard to athletics, track work begins tomorrow. There is to be a track meet later on between the four companies and the company which wins has special privileges. I shall try to lope over the hurdle I guess. Although I can't beat anybody. I shall be interested in this preliminary training for the track team in the spring.

You may have seen the letter I wrote to Roger which told about my going to see Mrs. Murphy, etc. If you have I won't say anything. The boy across the corridor doesn't like it here and wants to resign already. . . . Is it hot at home? It's pretty good down here. I was very homesick for a while this morning but got some mail after chapel and feel better now. Butler is here now. He seems to be a very nice fellow. His mother is here and he introduced me as the one who beat him out in the competitive exam. He has a flute and we have played together once. It is about supper time now and I must be ready when the bell rings.

Affectionately,
Ellsworth

ANNAPOLIS MD JULY 13 1909

Dear Mother

I got your letter yesterday which said you were going to Hartford and thought of you as being in a pretty nice place which I won't see for quite a while. As long as I do something I am all right, but as soon as I get time to cogitate, I get homesick. As you may know, I started "Great Expectations" when I was at home, so yesterday I went over to the library and got it out. I have read over 50 pages in my spare time since then. I was afraid that my opportunity to read a lot that I ought to read had gone, but I see that I can accomplish a great deal this summer. . . .

Last night we were awakened by a great noise and a shouting of "turn out." We had to get down into the rotunda and line up. Then the roll was called of each company. It was about the middle of the night just when we were very sound asleep. The officers down there thought it was a good joke, I guess but it failed to appeal to my sense of humor. Most of the fellows thought that there was a big fire somewhere but after a while they sent us back to bed. I guess somebody had been trying to French out and they wanted to find if every one was there. A week before I came they had a big fire down by the football grounds and all the middies had to go. It was 2 o clock Sunday morning. An officer found a man all burned and charred beyond recognition. He made a great fuss and called for an ambulance. The corpse was found to be a football tackling dummy.

We have systematic dumbbell drill every night in gym and have to run a quarter after it.

My vaccination didn't take and I can go swimming now. I look forward to mail time every day as the best part of the whole business. We had watermelon for dessert yesterday. . . .

Hoping to hear from you soon.

I remain sincerely

Your affectionate son,

Ellsworth

US NAVAL ACADEMY ANNAPOLIS MD JULY 27 1909

Dear Father,

I was glad to hear that you had 2 such nice days in Hampton. Mother told me about the drive to Westminster and Scotland. It is against the rules for midshipmen to ride in any vehicle whatsoever and sometimes I feel as if I should like to be driving some horses. What was the success of Emily Ellsworth's play?

The regular Naval Academy Marine Band is here but we don't get much chance to hear it. They practice every morning and we hear them while we are marching to the 10 a.m. drill. The other day they were playing The Merry Widow Waltz and it was hard to keep step to. They don't pay any attention to plebes evidently. Plebes are not allowed to use any of the benches along the walks in the yard either, so when they do have a band concert we don't get much benefit from it.

I don't believe I'll ever make much of a success of fencing. I can box better. I'm not doing much with the hurdles either. I haven't the requisite steam. Did I tell you that the top of the mast was 138' from the deck? Did you ever read "A double barreled Detective Story"?

Very affectionately,

Ellsworth

ANNAPOLIS MD SEPTEMBER 23 1909

Dear Mother,

I was O.D. yesterday as I expected. It is quite a job. You ought to have seen me inspecting the mess hall servants. Thirty big and little negroes had to stand in line at attention while I walked in front of them to see if they were all right. It seemed rather funny to me but they didn't find it out, because I frowned and looked as solemn and serious as possible. I wore a sword all day and ate my meals at the officer's table in the center. I also had to keep the log and inspect the milk. There were seven five gallon cans of milk and I had to drink some from each one. Wouldn't Roger like that job? There were lots of other things to be done but they wouldn't be interesting. That is the second time I have missed liberty by being on duty.

I started this letter before French but couldn't finish it. It is now just before dinner. Father's letter came yesterday and I was glad to hear that my letter got there before Ralph Risley did. The swimming drill from 5–6 has been discontinued and we get put out of the building every day from 5–6:30 to engage in athletic exercises. I generally go to gym first and being kicked out of there at 5:40 either visit the canteen or loaf around getting fat. I have gained only about twelve pounds.

Affectionately,
Ellsworth

ANNAPOLIS MD DECEMBER 5 1909

Dear Mother

. . . After much deliberation I bought a banjo. It cost $8.00 (second hand) and sounds pretty well. It can't possibly interfere with the studying for, as you know, there are certain study hours when no noise at all can be made. Outside of study hours we are not allowed to study. A fellow came to my room this afternoon while I was playing the violin and picked out a lot of my pieces for me to play to him. But there are a good many times when there are two or three odd minutes when there's scarcely time to take my violin out of the case and start to play, when I get a lot of comfort out of the banjo which has no case and which keeps in tune very well. I hope you're not mad because I got it, for I really get a lot of pleasure from it. . . .

Affectionately,
Ellsworth

US NAVAL ACADEMY DECEMBER 27 1909

Dear Cousin Lucy,

I thank you very much for your Christmas letter and the wherewithal to purchase some frivolity. We had great fun here Christmas, for the plebes took charge of things and treated the first classmen the same way that the first classmen usually treat them. That was a great relief, but one of the first classmen whom we treated pretty badly is getting even now.

I had my Christmas dinner at the Clark's where I went on Thanksgiving. Mrs. Clark is lovely. She smiles at me in chapel every Sunday morning. I never told Mother this but I don't believe she cares anyway.

It snowed here nearly all day Christmas and some more today. My roommate says he can't see how the snow stays here so long. It melts in two or three hours in Louisville, he says. I got a letter from Esther Saturday in which she said she was going on a skating party with Dean tonight. So I guess she's skating now. Please give her my best if you meet her in the drug store or anywhere.

Very affectionately,
Ellsworth

APRIL 27 1910

Dear Mother,

. . . There was quite an excitement Monday. A lieutenant, who owns an automobile, was driving around the yard with a woman. She was managing the wheel. They came around the gym pretty fast and almost struck a telegraph pole. She dodged the pole very neatly but then turned the wrong way and shot right off the sea wall into about ten feet of water. A 3 striper dove in after the woman and the lieutenant got out as best he could, but a poor little dog, chained to the car, had to stay below and drown. . . .

Very affectionately,
Ellsworth

DECEMBER 7 1910

Dear Mother,

We have had quite a storm, the most snow since I have been here. It began to snow Sunday night and didn't knock off until last night. All last winter we never had snow on the ground more than two days at a time.

For drill Monday and Tuesday the youngsters of this division had [to] work in the blacksmith shop. A man showed us how to forge iron and weld and Tuesday we had to do it ourselves. It is pretty strenuous work and I wouldn't want it for a steady. We had to take a piece of round iron, heat it white hot and then hammer it square. Then we had to make an L. It was quite a job to make a good right angle with a sharp corner.

Drill was over about 5 and on Monday the snow was just right, not wet, but just sticky enough and we had a glorious snowball fight in the yard all the way from the Steam Building to Bancroft Hall. Yesterday it was very cold and today was lovely.

Most of the fellows who didn't have enough lung capacity in the strength test have been put on a squad that has to meet at 5 o clock on Tuesday and take a "slow jogging run from 1 to 4 miles, walking occasionally for respiratory purposes." This is supposed to bring up the lungs. In this company 10 out of 15 youngsters hit the weak squad, which is to meet Thursdays and Fridays. Ralph Risley hit it. All but two of the 10th Co 1st classmen hit it. George Lowry 3 striper among others. A great many who were considered strong last year are on so it isn't any disgrace to be on it. The champion hammer thrower is there and our left end on the football team is one of the merry bunch, so I would feel rather left out of it had I lost my place in its ranks.

Very affectionately,
Ellsworth

OCTOBER 12 1911

Dear Father,

If a fellow learned all the lessons they handed out second class year, he would have an education sure enough. Incomprehensible! If they are that to you, I'd hate to say what they are to me. Yesterday there was great rejoicing around here for the plumbers at last got the pipes fixed and the low shower was turned on. This may be the sunny south but those cold showers were something fierce. Now, however, we have "beaucoup de l'eau chaud" which is a great luxury.

There is a regulation around here now that we cannot whistle in the corridors. This place is supposed to be run as far as practicable like a battleship so, as we cannot whistle aboard ship, they are beginning by forbidding it now.

The O.C. asked Keisker what he stood this morning when he came in to inspect. He said six and then the O.C. asked me. I said 100 to which he replied, "well that's more like what I stood." Guess he'll spoon on me now. Did I write that we have the Ass't O.C. living directly across the corridor from us? They made Wilson and Quinlan move out so he could move in.

We won our first game Saturday 27–5. They blocked a punt and managed to drop on it behind our line, thus scoring by a fluke. It was Johns Hopkins. Yesterday we beat the St. Johnnies 21–0. Saturday we play Washington and Jefferson and 7 days is at Colonial. Keisker has seen it and says it is very good.

I have read the book "When a man Marries." Henderson is getting along very well at the U of Wis. studying farming. Ray Covel is married. I must go to dinner and bone after that until bed time. "Life at the US Naval Academy is one continuous round of pleasure, sir," as the plebes say at the table. Much love to Mother and Dorothy.

As ever,
Ellsworth

OCTOBER 15 1911

Dear Mother,

Carl and Ethel are coming here next Saturday to spend the night at Carvel Hall. Won't it be fine for me to have them here. That is the day of the Princeton game which will be quite an attraction. It is to be played on the new field over by the armory between the Armory and the sea wall where they have a fine new stand seating 10,000. There is a hop that night which will bring lots of girls and I guess Ethel will think it a pretty gay place.

Two of my classmates and some youngsters were caught hazing and have received 100 demerits each, restricted until December 1, which means they lose the game and lose all September leave 1912. Isn't that dreadful?

This regulation forbidding whistling is pretty easy to forget. Every little while some one starts up a tune and the M.C. pipes up, "Knock off that whistling." This will be a pretty mournful place as that was one of the chief diversions to help you forget your troubles. I have received your two letters since I wrote last and was very happy to have them.

Principles of Mechanisms is the hardest thing I ever saw, but another week has passed without seeing me in the tree. The exams are always terrible though.

I could come near to starring if I were a plebe now. They don't have any mechanical drawing but 5 periods of English and five of Dago (instead of 3 each) per week and six of math. That would just about suit me. . . .

This is a cold rainy day and I hope you are having a better one. You haven't said anything about coming down to Philadelphia but I hope so very, very much that you'll come. It seems long months since I left you. Well, please give my love to the family and keep all you want for yourself.

Very affectionately,
Ellsworth

NOVEMBER 2 1911

Dear Mother,

I am so very very sorry that you and Father cannot come to Philly on the 25th. I have had four tickets sent Father, two of which he can send to Carl. Maybe Richard Lyman could come down with Roger, unless he is going to Cambridge for their big game. If he is going to the Hahvahd game, would it be possible for Wolcott to come down? I would very much like to have one of them go.

Ring worm has been quite widespread here for the past three weeks but the epidemic is now about over. I have developed it now however, and had to move out yesterday to have my room fumigated. This is the best room in the building, a study room and two bedrooms, eight windows altogether, commanding the finest views, both up the river and up and down the bay. I am living alone. Keisker being over in 462. He is not isolated and goes to recitations but I am on the sick list, can sleep through reveille if I want and take a nap when I feel so inclined. It's fine. There is only one other with the "leprosy", a plebe from Alabama by the name of Wood. I spoon on him and we all get along very well together. His brother graduated at Yale Law last year. I don't know how long I'll be here, but it's fine to have the rest. . . . I do so wish that you could come to the game, and feel very sorry that Father is not well. The boys are just coming back from seamanship recitation and I guess I'll look at a little Mechanics. It is getting worse and worse, but coming out sat the first month is very encouraging with 35 unsat.

Very lovingly,
Ellsworth

JANUARY 6 1912

Dear Father,

Yesterday the brigade went to Washington for Admiral Evan's funeral. It was the coldest day I can remember since I have been here. We had lunch at 10:25 and left Annapolis via W.B. and A special about 11:30 with overcoats and leggings and underarms and underclothes, too. It was a very slow trip, the cars stopping every little while. It seemed too cold for the electricity. We finally arrived in Washington at nearly 3 o clock and immediately marched to Arlington. Going through Washington and Georgetown was bad enough but when we crossed the Arlington bridge, the wind that swept down the Potomac was some cold. Lots of the boys had their ears and noses frozen. After getting into Arlington we lined up and the rest of the funeral procession passed. The band played Nearer My God to Thee and we stood at present arms while the body of "Fighting Bob", on a caveson drawn by six horses, went by. Then we came back, arriving here at 7:45. Our company was the first one back and the 5th and 6th came along soon after, but a car was derailed and the rest of the brigade didn't arrive until nearly 10 o clock. All hands were departed in Math this morning as a result. . . .

Affectionately,
Ellsworth

OCTOBER 10 1912

Dear Father,

It's a long time since I left home now, and I haven't even written to you. Well, as I wrote Uncle Pierre, it's great! This 1st Class year is something I wouldn't miss for a great deal. I'm in love as bad as ever, worse if possible, but then you never saw such a change in the point of view which the last lap brings. I play my violin, and in this big bare room the tone has a chance to get out and sounds fine.

Then we have our large smoking hall with a very good Victor at one end with lots of fine records and a piano at the other end. The fellows have a very sociable and enjoyable time there. All the brigade officers have received commissions signed by the Supe and the Com. I got mine today. It gives a spiel about their reposing trust and confidence in our fidelity and ability. It's about the size of that appointment I gave you.

I am on the swimming squad, not the non-swimmers (analogous to the weak squad) but the academy one. That is so I don't have to take a cross country walk on Thursday afternoon for drill. I battled Dago today. Tomorrow there is Naval Construction, Navigation, Torpedoes, Drill and Physiology and Hygiene on the program. I guess I'll take a little exercise, play a little music and write a couple of letters too on the side. Oh, there's nothing like it. I hear they're going to send us to gunboats after graduation instead of battleships. Wonder if it's true. Please give my love to Mother and Roger when you see him.

Affectionately,
Ellsworth

MARCH 5 1913

Dear Mother,

The celebration is over. I didn't hear reveille at all yesterday but woke up in time to hear 4 bells. Breakfast formation was at 6:05 and we left at

7:30. Upon disembarking in Washington at the B & O some one rushed up to me, calling me by name. The cadet trains were right next to ours and this was one of the cadets, Warren Weisheimer. Do you know him? We talked about all our friends coming out. . . .

Then we marched off to the Capitol where we lined up in columns of companies, facing the corps. We were very near the President's stand but could not hear what he said. Bryan was the man who received the ovation when he appeared. There wasn't one tenth the cheering for Wilson that there was for Bryan. After waiting about 1½ hours, the President came out and turned over the country to Wilson who made his speech and then the parade began. It was ten miles long. We couldn't see much of it but saw the crowds. We marched by over 600,000 people and received quite a few cheers. We had our overcoats on which were quite heavy before the end of the march, also the guns.

Then we were given a beautiful luncheon in Mr. McClean's beautiful home on Massachusetts Avenue. As we went in we all spoke first to Mrs. McClean who presented us to Admiral Dewey. The Admiral shook hands with every midshipman in the brigade. The first classmen dined upstairs. This was at 4:15, our first meal since 6:30 a.m. After marching 8 miles and being on our feet for six hours counting stops. We had grapefruit, bouillon, chicken salad, chicken croquettes, peas, spuds, bread, rolls, cakes, ice cream, coffee. It was very fine. And the orchestra of 30 pieces was one of the best I've heard in a long time. There were also some girls there and there was an informal dance after the luncheon. We then marched back to the station and arrived here at 9:30. I went on duty then after dinner as O.D. and had to write up the log. I finally had a bath and turned in. I've been on duty all day. We had a company dinner in Smoke Hall tonight to practice after dinner speaking. I wasn't called on. Please give my love to Father. I was very happy to receive your letter on my return from Washington.

Affectionately,
Ellsworth

MAY 28 1913

Dear Father,

No more rivers. Many's the time I thought I'd never live to see this happy day, but here it actually is. And that river this morning was some stream. There were not so many logs in it as in the Navigation exam, but it was nevertheless one that makes you feel thankful to have behind. It was the only one that had me scared and I battled it safely. To think that I am actually thru with the Department of Marine Engineering and Naval Construction in the USNA seems too good to be true, but true it is, and in three days from now my dear Father and Mother will be with me.

Tomorrow we get liberty from 1:15 to 5:30 and after dinner until 9:30. Friday, as I wrote to Mother, I expect to go on the Argo on a sailing party. The second half of the seamanship was a good square practical exam on Rules of the road and most of us made 4.0 on it.

Such a feeling of relief not to have to study—for I really have had to do more or less of that sort of thing during the past month. Please give my love to mother. I guess this will be about the last letter. Please give my love to Cousin Lucy and remember me to Esther.

Affectionately,
Ellsworth

CHAPTER 8

Dearest Audrey

The Letters of Orin Shepley Haskell

During his time at the Naval Academy, Orin Haskell wrote to his girlfriend, Audrey McDougall, about topics as mundane as the weather and as deadly as the influenza epidemic. In the following letters, the young Haskell, a native of Pittsfield, Maine, wrote to his hometown sweetheart, who became his first wife, Audrey, in 1921. He created cameos of academy life: "It is so hot here that if it were not for the breeze it would be unbearable. In chapel this morning it was so hot that to keep the back of my 'blouse' from clinging to the back of the seat, I put a prayer book behind me and sweat so that the red on the prayer book ran all over the back of my white blouse." When the lethal flu epidemic hit the academy, Orin, with many of his classmates, was hospitalized. "Four mids have died so far and some others are very sick." In another letter, he confided, "Last night we had a 'rough house' on the 4th floor and one of the boys had his head pushed through the pane of glass in one of the doors and was cut quite badly."

Serving the navy until 1924, Haskell retired as a lieutenant, junior grade. After a stint as headmaster at Lyman Abbott School in Farmington, Maine, Haskell went on to a thirty-year career at General Electric. He died on 26 June 1974.

AUGUST 5 1916

Dearest Audrey,

It is so hot here today that if it were not for the breeze it would be unbearable. In chapel this morning it was so hot that to keep the back of my "blouse" from clinging to the back of the seat, I put a prayer book behind me and sweat so that the red on the prayer book ran all over the

Orin Shepley Haskell
Courtesy The Lucky Bag */ USNA Nimitz Special Collections*

back of my white blouse (We call our coats blouses). It was so hot last night that I did not sleep more than an hour I guess. . . .

Yours, with love
O.S.H.

AUGUST 7 1916
Dearest Audrey,

Today is the first day we have shot the machine guns and it is a great sport. All you have to do is pull the trigger and a string of steel goes out of the barrel until you release the trigger. They shoot about 500 shots per minute. I made high score today but believe it was a mistake.

The first and second battalions changed rooms over into the other wing this afternoon, but as my room is not quite ready yet, we did not move so we have the whole right wing to ourselves tonight and it seems mighty quiet around.

Our wrestling instructor broke his arm this afternoon while carrying on a class in the gymnasium. It's too bad because we all liked him better than any other instructors we have.

We all get paid off Wednesday ($1) and they let us all go out in town Saturday. A dollar seems like a fortune here. If we need anything we can go to the store and get it without paying for it on requisition, but they allow us very little spending money. All we have to spend is a dollar a month and a dollar candy check. We really do not need any more though because all we have to spend it for is the movies. They pay us $2 a day while we are here at school but they keep most of it and we don't get it until graduation, as they expect every officer to have so much money when he graduates. I think it is a good plan. . . .

This has been another hot day but we have a fine breeze so I do not mind it very much. When we are out on dress parade we can guess about how the militia is feeling down in Mexico these hot days.

I believe they are going to give us a dance in town Saturday. I almost hope they don't as dancing in uniforms is too hard work in the summer.

Have not heard from you since Saturday but am living in hopes for tomorrow.

Yours, with love,
Whack

AUGUST 10, 1916

Dear Audrey,

. . . Last night we had a "rough house" on the 4th floor and one of the boys had his head pushed through the pane of glass in one of the doors and was cut quite badly. The executive officer found out about it after taps and called assembly, so we all had to turn out and have another pajama formation. By the time he had the names of all those who were in the "fracas" we were all mighty sleepy and glad to turn in again.

Did I tell you that we have sharks here in the bay? They have been driven here from southern waters on account of the changing of the course of the Gulf Stream or something of that sort, so when we go in swimming we have a squad of sharpshooters perched up on a height where they can see all the surface of the water around, and shoot any sharks that might make a dash for any of us in the water. They have seen none so far and jelly fish are our greatest trouble just now. . . .

It is time to get ready to go over to the gymnasium so, so long, for today.

Yours with love,
Whack

THURSDAY NIGHT

Dear Audrey,

That was surely a good joke about your getting that letter of Carter's as the joke seems to be on you and Carter himself rather than on me as he intended. You see it was like this: whenever a letter is mailed and discovered not to have a stamp on it, before it gets to the post office, the address on the letter is read out at formation in order that the writer may call at the office, get it, and remail it. Well Carter thought that it would be a good joke to mail a letter to you without a stamp and hear the following read out at formation: "Attention to orders. The midshipman who has mailed a letter to Miss Audrey McDougall, E. Boothbay, Maine, will call at the post office for the same to pay additional postage." He told a lot of fellows about it so they all intended to laugh when it was read out and attract attention to me, so everyone would know I sent it, and have the laugh on me. But, it seems that the letter got to the P.O. and was finally sent to you.

Several fellows were found to be cheating in marking high scores at the rifle range, so tonight we all had to sign a paper saying we had not cheated in our own scores and knew of no one who had cheated. I'm afraid several middies will have to leave as they have no use for a cheat here. . . .

Our battalion won the wrestling last night but lost the boxing, so unless we can win the track meet Saturday, we are lost.

Yours, with love,
O.S.H.

Reina Mercedes, the prison ship. "Did I tell you that Carter is on the prison ship for two weeks? He and several other fellows were caught smoking and had to move over on the *Reina Mercedes.*" *Courtesy USNA Nimitz Library Archives*

FRIDAY EVENING

Dear Audrey,

. . . A terrible order was published here this noon—from our viewpoint, at least. Several cases of infantile paralysis have been reported in Annapolis, so Captain Eberle issued an order that no midshipmen will be allowed outside of the grounds and closed Bancroft Hall to visitors. All children are excluded from the Academy. Now, the paralysis itself is bad enough but when it comes just at a weekend and over Labor Day when we have a holiday it makes us all just a little peeved. . . .

Did I tell you that Carter is on the prison ship for two weeks? He and several other fellows were caught smoking and had to move over on the Reina Mercedes. They say they don't mind it any, but you can imagine about how much they enjoy sleeping in hammocks or being confined on deck all during recreation hours. Of course, it isn't like a real prison ship, but is used to isolate the midshipmen when they do something that the commandant thinks reflects on the honor of the service. The Reina Mercedes is a Spanish cruiser captured in the War of 1898. . . . I guess you have heard about enough of our "doins" so good night.

Yours, with love,
OSH

SUNDAY NOON (OCT 15?) 1916

Dearest Audrey,

We had a fire here this afternoon which partly demolished one of the artillery sheds. The fire siren blew right after lunch and we all had to go just as we were in our dress uniforms, as it is a rule that all midshipmen must go to a fire on the grounds immediately in whatever uniform they may have on. We got mighty wet, and look like drowned rats. I expect the tailors will have a fine time pressing our uniforms before next Sunday. Two midshipmen were cut by falling glass but no one was hurt seriously.

One funny thing happened. Captain Nulton, the commandant, was standing nearby in full dress uniform with all his gold braid on. Suddenly a bunch of us ran around the corner with a fire hose and turned it full force on him. It took him off his feet and sat him very ungracefully in the middle of a mud puddle, much to the detriment of his uniform. Of course, it was an accident! (?) . . .

Yours, with love,
O.S.H.

NOVEMBER 10, 1916

Dearest Audrey,

. . . There is great excitement here now over the football game on the 25th. We have a big crowd out at practice every evening. I suppose you have heard the Navy mascot is a goat and the Army's is a mule. We have the goat out for practice every night tied in front of the bleachers. Tonight he got away and it took the whole bunch of us about twenty minutes to catch him. It was a good deal like a greased pig contest.

I hear tonight that Wilson is re-elected by 17 votes but that Wilcox has demanded a recount. I suppose it will not really be decided for a week or so yet. I wish Hughes had been elected because I don't relish the idea of standing at attention for an hour to hear Wilson's inauguration in March. . . .

Yours, with love,
O.S.H.

NOVEMBER 17, 1916

Dearest Audrey,

Tomorrow we have the last game before "the game." . . . We have a snake dance every night now after dinner. We have a song we sing down in the dining room. You see there are about 60 tables and one table down at one end sings then the next table and so on right around. It sounds like a big wind coming up and passing on (Dramatic)

"Away, away with sword and drum,
Here we come, here we come,
Looking for someone to put on the bum,
We're got to beat the Army."

There are about a hundred other verses, but this happens to be one that comes for our table. They all end "we've got to beat the Ar—m—my!" . . . I think you've caught the Navy spirit for the football game. There isn't a middie here who wouldn't give his right hand to win. We got beat last year and everyone was crying when he got off the train coming back. It's almost as much as life and death to us. The Army has a wonderful team but we shall have all the more honor to whip them.

Liberty for plebes tomorrow but not for me as I am on conduct grade. I have special permission to go out though until 4 pm and after dinner until 9:30 PM

Had a bunch of corn growers or something down here to see us drill today. It was the worst looking bunch of hicks I've seen for some time.

Yours, with love,
O.S.H.

NOVEMBER 21, 1916

Dearest Audrey,

. . . The football team leaves Thursday evening. My roommate is on the team and I tried to get a job as "water boy" or something but there was nothing doing, so I have to wait and go on Saturday with the regiment. It is mighty hard to study this week with all the excitement going on—in fact—nobody is studying. We talk all the time about the game and if the "gray legs" trim us this year there will be h– to pay. . . .

We are practicing now a special drill to give in New York on the Polo Grounds. We form in battalion fronts . . . and then break up into columns of companies just before we take the stands. We shall have to wear overcoats as it will be cold, so it will not look as well as it would in "dress."

The goat we had as mascot died day before yesterday. I don't know whether that is good luck or not. We've got another goat and hope to see him drive the Army mule way off the field. You see they introduce the mule and the goat before the game and three years ago, the goat got loose and butted the mule all over the grounds—and Navy won 3 to 0.

There is too much to do today to write very long letters but [I] shall write longer ones after the game.

Yours, with love,
O.S.H.

FRIDAY EVENING

Dearest Audrey,

The team left last night at 5 and we leave tomorrow morning at 5:50 A.M. I have just come back from the last recitation, and all we have to do now is draw the money for the trip. We are allowed only $10 outside of our carfare and hotel bill, but we have been saving up for some time so we have a small fortune together.

We all went out to the train and as we were not in ranks we raised h– in general. Consequently, we can never go out with the team again. Hard luck! I hate to think of crawling out of bed at 4 a.m. but I guess I can do it for one day. Just came in from drill. We practiced taking the stands again today.

Yours, with love,
O.S.H.

SUNDAY EVENING

Dearest Audrey,

This is a mighty sad crowd around here tonight. I suppose you know that Army beat us and if you have read any of the New York papers you know all about how the game was played. For my part I hate to even think of the game. It's no fun to have an Army victory and have to stand up before 50,000 people with hats off and let the "graylegs" hoot at us after the game. We shall get them next year just the same. . . .

Last night we had a good time in New York—as good as we could have under the circumstances and the way we felt. We stayed at the Manhattan and they surely treated us white. We went to the Hippodrome which was all decorated in Navy colors on one side and Army colors on the other. They gave a special act for our benefit as nearly all the cadets and middies were there. The first scene was a building at West Point and the ballet was all dressed as cadets and sang "Benny Haven O"—the West Point song. Then the next scene was here and the ballet in middie uniforms singing "Anchors Aweigh"—believe me we lifted the roof. They had a very good show including Anna Pavlova—the great Russian dancer and the ice ballet. After the show we got a party and went to Rector's. All the tables were taken or reserved but one of the men who had reserved a table offered to let us have it and we gladly accepted—you bet. Everywhere we went the band was playing "Anchors Aweigh" and we sang until we were hoarse. We stayed at Rector's until 3:30 a.m., so we are some sleepy tonight. It is only 8:30 now but I am going to turn in as soon as I finish this.

We had a record crowd at the game and New York just opened up and gave us a swell time. It was generally conceded that our drilling was much better than West Point. In fact one paper, The Herald, said the West Pointers looked seedy "as if they had fallen into their clothes" . . . We were a sleepy sour bunch at dinner tonight and it will take some time to get over this defeat. It may seem foolish but after the game we all cried like babies. It is one of the biggest social events of the year in New York and we certainly made the most of it. . . . I'm so sleepy that I shall go to sleep writing this if I don't look out, so good night.

Yours, with love,

O.S.H.

SEPTEMBER 22 1918

Dearest Audrey

. . . Rather a sad thing happened to us today as the brother of my roommate, who is a lieutenant in the Navy, died last night of Spanish influenza, which has had such a run in the Navy and especially the northern states. It was mighty hard as he was a splendid officer and has been flag officer of the Pacific fleet for the past year. He had just been married and has a small baby. He graduated from here in 1915. As his brother said "He is only one in a million whom we shall lose" but it seemed hard for such a fine fellow to die just as he is needed so much. And they say that the Germans introduced the disease into this country. This is one thing more to hate them for. I did not hate the German people at the beginning of the war but certainly do now and if I ever get a chance to kill a German I shall kill him good. . . .

Write often, dear, and please forget rain, sun and tide. This is a blunt way to say it but can't we make our letters a little more personal. Remember me to your folks when you write and walk down Congress Street once just for me.

With love,
OSH

OCTOBER 6 1918

Dearest Audrey,

You are probably saying all kinds of disagreeable things about me for not writing for the last two weeks, but you see your box of fudge came and made me so sick that I could not write. Really though Audrey, it was mighty fine of you to send that candy and it was great. I did not open it until I got back from the hospital yesterday and as it was about two weeks old I imagined that it would be no good, but it had kept fine and tasted like fresh fudge.

Perhaps you have heard that the influenza has us here. We have had 1000 cases and four deaths so far. The fellow in the next bed to me in the hospital passed on. He was a fellow from Georgia and as he was a Scotchman was a mighty fine chap.

I was mighty surprised to get your letter saying that all the Portland schools are closed and that you are at home. I only hope the flu doesn't get you. If you get the influenza, get in bed and keep covered as if your life depended on it as it is very easy to catch pneumonia and if you get that it is "good night". The main thing is not to get cold. . . .

You say that you saw in the paper that there will be an Army Navy game but everybody around here says there is no hope. . . .

We are beginning to get dope about early graduation but I guess that we shall be right here until next June. They are going to graduate a class at West Point in December sometime. . . .

Have a lot of work to make up so cannot write long. Be careful and do not get the flu and remember that I am

Yours, with love,
O.S.H.

OCTOBER 7 1918

Dearest Audrey

It seems like an unusually long time since I have had a letter from you but I suppose that the time is dragging up simply because I am not doing anything. Since I came back from the hospital Saturday I have been to no recitations as they are keeping me on the sick list although I am feeling fine aside from a slight cold. I think that I shall begin to do regular work on Wednesday. Fours mids have died so far and some others are very sick. The flu is having a big run and is hitting them much harder in some places than it has us here. Even the postmaster has the flu because the mail hasn't come yet. . . .

As soon as I get back to work maybe I can get up pep enough to write a real letter so shall try again as soon as I hear from you.

Yours, with love,
O.S.H.

OCTOBER 27 1918

Dearest Audrey,

The quarantine was lifted today with a bang. Liberty, football game with Newport Training School—we won 47–7—and a big hop last night. There was not much of anything to do on liberty as all movie houses, etc do not open until next Saturday, but there was a big crowd down for the football game and hop and some of our airmen amused us between halves with a little trick flying. . . .

This forenoon I was on duty at the gate and I never realized before how many unreasonable old women there are in the world. My orders were to allow no one to go to Bancroft Hall without an escort by a midshipman on duty and to let no one go in to the chapel until 10:30 A.M. Every woman who came in "just couldn't understand" why she couldn't see her son if she wanted to, or go to chapel as she saw fit for "she wasn't going to blow the place up." Of course, I could only tell them that that was my orders and let it go at that, but with about fifty women to hold back for an hour I had a merry time and am nearly a mental wreck this afternoon for answering so many foolish questions. The men were all different. All you have to do is tell them that they can't come in and that satisfies them but I guess that all women like to argue about so much. . . .

I am planning on going out in town today awhile so hope you will call this a letter. . . .

Yours with love,
O.S.H.

NOVEMBER 12 1918

Dearest Audrey

As I am feeling unusually savvy today as I finished a two hour exam in Navigation in one hour I will use part of the other hour with you.

You should have seen the celebration here yesterday in Annapolis. You know the people down here don't know how to celebrate the way we do up north and haven't any more pep than a lot of old women. Hoddie and I walked into town yesterday as there was no drill and saw what we thought to be a funeral procession coming down the street, but when we came near we found out that it was Annapolis trying to celebrate the signing of the armistice. How anyone can spend a lifetime in this town is more than I can see. Why E. Boothbay is a howling metropolis side of this place. The census man says that 10,000 people live here, but I believe that most of them are in the graveyard . . . had better quit until next time.

Yours, with much love,
O.S.H.

NOVEMBER 14 1918

Dearest Audrey

You would have had a good laugh tonight if you had seen me trying to make an after dinner speech. You see our last year here we have a course in after dinner speaking which consists of having a dinner each week in Memorial Hall at which twenty of us have to attend. An English prof presides as toastmaster and after we have filled ourselves up to our utmost capacity for they give us a regular "blood" feed—they call on four or five at random for after dinner speeches on various subjects. Mine tonight was supposed to be on "naval autocracy" and I was supposed to be the commanding officer at the transport "Martha Washington" on her way home from France and speaking to a bunch of army officers whom I had invited to dinner. Well that would have been alright if I had known anything about the subject but am afraid that my efficiency mark will look something like this—0—this month.

Last night the commandant had a meeting with my class and told us that unless we did much better work from now on than we have been doing this year, we would have to stay here two more years instead of one, and instead of graduating in June, a year from June. I believe that he is just trying to scare us into a little more work but still he can do it if he wants to. Also he said that whether we had Christmas leave or not depended entirely upon how much work we do between now and Christmas.

Yesterday I had a letter from mother written in bed saying that she was sick and did not know when she can come to Annapolis. Charles wrote me that she is very sick and of course I am more than worried about her. You know she was in the big Bar Harbor accident when the wharf gave way and drowned about 30 people. She was hurt at that time and has never really gotten over it. However, I am hoping that she will be a lot better soon, and I shall hear that she is up and around again in a day or so.

Your last letters sounded hopeful for a visit to Annapolis so am hoping that you can come soon—the sooner the better. . . .

Yours, with love,
O.S.H.

NOVEMBER 21, 1918

Dear Audrey,

Am on duty today but by some freak of good fortune hit a deck here in Bancroft Hall instead of officer of the day at the Barracks. I say by good fortune because as officer of the day there is so much to do that there is no time to either study or write letters or anything of the sort, while here in Bancroft Hall all we have to do is sit at a desk and as there is nothing to do except make inspections once in a while, it is "fruit" for us. If the duty officer were not a good natured chap I would not attempt to write this letter on duty, but if he inquires about it I can call it a theme so that will make it all right anyway.

Just now I am considering the marine corps very seriously. When I wrote you something about it before you said that you did not think much of the marines but did not know why. Now the chief reason I want to get into the marines is because I hate engineering duty so much. The idea of having to stand watches below decks on a battleship in the fireroom or engine room as we have had to do the last two summers is almost unbearable to me. I don't like that work and if by chance I should be detailed for that duty after graduation I should be in absolute misery every watch I had to stand. Of course, if I could have above deck work, navigation, ordnance, etc, I would like that, but at some time or other everyone gets engineering duty. Now in the marines, it is all topside work and while there is not the chance of learning as much as there is in the regular navy, still it is an easy life and a very pleasant one. In fact the main trouble with life for a marine officer is that he does not have enough to do. In time of peace he has nothing to do but draw his pay and hold a drill once a day or something like that, so there is a tendency for a fellow to get into a rut after awhile. The work, though, that they have to do is the kind that I like, and I believe more and more that it is what I want to do. The hard part of it is after all not making up my mind to do it, but in getting permission to do it. You see about a hundred in my class all want to get into the Marines and they have begun to turn back requests for the marine corps. . . .

O.S.H.

DECEMBER 1 1918

Dearest Audrey,

Please excuse this paper as I am absolutely out of stationery and have not time to go out in town for any.

It seems like a crime to let good weather such as we are having here today go wasted. Now if you were only here or I were in Portland we could take a long walk or something. It seems a shame all right because—well as you once said we are never young but once and by the time we poor mids ever get situated where we can take walks when, where, and with whom we want, we shall be so old that we shall have to ride. Did you ever stop to think Audrey how many good times people have to miss just to do something that they really don't want to do? And the trouble with this infernal school is that it takes all the ambition—that is all the ambition to be of some good in the world—out of a man. I haven't anymore ambition left than a cow and feel more worthless everyday. This school may turn out good officers for the navy but that is the only thing we shall be of any use as. If I should leave the service I am so worthless that I could not make $10 a week at a ribbon counter and hold down my job.

Anyway I am handing in my request for a commission in the Marine Corps after I graduate, so shall not have to worry that any longer. They may send me to Java or Indo China or someplace like that but I don't care where I go as long as I get away from this infernal Annapolis.

I often wish that I had gone to a regular college instead of here, as we certainly miss a lot of good times and have to work harder for an education than any school I know of, and then after four years, all we have learned is how to order somebody else around. Well, I guess that will be enough of my troubles for one day. One thing more though—Josephus was down here today and was standing directly in front of my company at inspection. After calling the roll I thought I would do an exceptionally snappy about face to show off and nearly broke my neck doing it, much to the extreme pleasure of the company.

Write me all about your week at home because my visits on paper with you are the most pleasant part of these days.

With much love,

O.S.H.

CHAPTER 9

I Called Him a Draft Dodger

The Letters of Daniel Vincent Gallery

"You also said I was a bum and that a bum is a person completely lacking in all principles of manhood." With these words, Midshipman Gallery took strong exception to an epistolary reprimand from his father, emphatically defending his honor.

Emphatic defense became somewhat of a Gallery trademark. In December 1918 he gained notoriety when in a fight he knocked out Worth B. Daniels, class of 1922, a son of the secretary of the navy. Daniels had chosen to resign. When Gallery called him a draft dodger, Daniels challenged him to a fight and Gallery accepted the challenge. Due in part to Daniels's famous father, the fight caught the public imagination and made headlines across the nation.

Although Gallery was guilty of no wrongdoing, the newspapers scrutinized him. The young man's strength of character, which allowed him to endure this particular storm, was a central ingredient in his personality. The details of his life—his Olympic wrestling, his stellar naval career, his prolific publications—continue to be explored and written about.

In these letters, we see a glimpse of the Chicago native who entered the academy at sixteen. We hear his strong views about everything from hazing to the lethal flu epidemic. His religious observances are evident throughout these letters, as he routinely informs his parents when he is able to attend Mass and when events prevent that attendance.

When Gallery died in 1977, the newspaper headlines referred to him as the "Commander of Carrier That Captured U-boat" and the "Author of Humorous Stories of Navy." His fame rests on his military service and his writing talent. These letters capture the beginnings of both.

Daniel Vincent Gallery
Courtesy The Lucky Bag/*USNA Nimitz Special Collections*

SEPTEMBER 16 1917

Dear Papa,

I will change my address next Wednesday to room 358 Marine Barracks. 250, from the plebe class only, are going over there. I would give almost anything to stay here but we have no choice. There will be 24 of us in a room or sort of dormitory. They are going to put up screens for partitions and thus divide it up into 12 "rooms" with 2 in a room. Koops will be in the same big room that I will be but he will not be my real roommate. I have only met the fellow who will be my roommate once. His name is Cook and I think he is a bilger though I don't know for sure. That is all I know about him now.

I got papped again last week for not having my shoes shined and having my neckerchief on wrong. The Duty Officer told the Assistant Duty Officer to put me down for untidiness of dress which is 3 D's. The O.D. made a mistake and put me down for unmilitary conduct which can bring me from 3 to 10 D's. If I only get 3 D's I will let it go but if they give me more than that I will call attention to the mistake. . . .

I heard that we may only be in the barracks for two months. I hope this is true. It will be fine for two months but not any longer. If we were to be there all year we would not be real members of the class because while there we will only come into the Academic limits for four hours a week. All our studies except Mech Drawing will be had over there. We would not know any upperclassmen nor the members of our own class if we were there all year. We would not get run but because of that we might not rate running next year. I would gladly take running if I could stay here. The running is part of the life here and even though we don't admit it, it is fun for us too. . . .

Dan

SEPTEMBER 23, 1917

Dear Papa,

Now that we are settled here in the barracks it doesn't seem to be such a terrible place after all. There is not an upperclass man living here and hence it is called plebe heaven. We hear harrowing reports of what is happening over in Bancroft every day. But there is one cloud in the sky. The first class duty squad comes on tonight and there will be a first class squad here all year. It won't be half as bad as at Bancroft but I don't believe it will be very dull. . . .

Dan.

SEPTEMBER 30,1917

Dear Papa,

We are having one awful time over here in the barracks. We do not get run like the fellows at Bancroft do; we get papped instead. Our pap sheets over here are huge compared with those across the creek. Here we have an average of 100 paps a day (putting it low) and over at Bancroft where they have six times as many to pap, they average 10 a day. I hit the pap five times last week; the fellow that rooms next to me hit it five times this morning. I am trying to be just as reg as I can and in fact nearly everyone is but we get papped right and left just the same. As least I have not been nailed for the same thing twice. They may get me once for a lot of things—once but once is all. . . .

I did not go to Communion today as there was a mistake in making out the call list and I was not called in time. I went to High Mass with a regular party. There were about 150 went to High Mass. . . .

I think it is due to the mail system in the barracks that you got my letter late. They only have one collection a day.

Dan.

SEPTEMBER 21, 1918

Dear Papa,

I am in the hospital now, supposed to have Spanish influenza. They shipped me over here yesterday morning. I was not feeling very bad when I got here and the doc said he expected to send me back today but he has postponed it till tomorrow morning now. I am feeling o.k. now except that I am three quarters starved. They have us on a liquid diet now consisting of one cup of milk and one cup of so called chicken broth a day. The next time I come over here I am going to buy all the chocolate bars I can lay my hands on and smuggle them in with me. There are about 33 of us over here now with the flu. The epidemic started last week and spread so fast that the hospital cannot hold another man. The whole Academy is quarantined on account of it.

I brought my books along with me but a fellow can't do much boning on this diet. I am as hungry as a bear all the time.

Dan.

SEPTEMBER 29, 1918

Dear Papa,

The doc decided not to turn me loose when Friday morning arrived. However, he promised to let me out Saturday morning. When thinking it over Saturday morning he said we'll let you out Sunday for sure. This morning he came around and said stick around again so here I am in bed.

I don't know how much longer they are going to keep me here but I don't put much confidence in what the sawbones says anymore. When I was just about to die of starvation yesterday they brought around some real solid chow. I have had four meals of what they call soft diet. That would amount to about one real meal.

I am not feeling really sick at all but I am not yet all the way back in my normal orbit.

There were no chapel services today and as usual dope got busy right away. They say the epidemic of flu is raising the dickens so much at the hall that they are going to knock off studies for a week. It sounds too good to be true. If they did that I could catch up with them over here and savvy my stuff better than if I had never been laid up at all.

As it is I am pretty close on their heels in calc, skinny and history. Since there are no exams in dago and mech and since one week's work does not depend upon the week before, I do not have to pay so much attention to those two. There is no way of finding weekly marks except by getting them from the tree. This is not a very good way for obvious reasons. The best I can do in regard to weekly marks is to guess.

Continue to address me at Bancroft Hall as I get my letters over here by the next delivery. The hospital is closer to the Hall than the Barracks.

Dan.

OCTOBER 6 1918

Dear Papa,

I got back from the hospital last Tuesday. Since then I have been turned in in my room with nothing to do but sleep and wander in the mess hall for chow if I wanted chow. No formations to attend, no recitations, taps and reveille meant nothing. Koops was in the same fix. Exactly half the regiment were turned in in this way and unable to study for at least four or five days and still the pigheaded academic department would not knock off work.

This put us all quite a lot behind but I have managed to catch up in nearly everything. In calc I am up to Monday's lesson. I am not finding that hard. Dago and steam are both so taught that you can let back and slide when in the hospital and not suffer in the least. I read nearly the whole of the naval history book in the hospital and they have dropped the exam this month so I am o.k. in that. I have put in about seven hours on skinny (physics) and intend to give it two hours tonight so I hope to be o.k. in that too. On the whole I don't think my marks will suffer from my spell of flu.

The hospital was filled up with flu patients before the epidemic got fairly started so they had to start turning fellows in in their rooms. The corridors looked like small streets during election time there were so many small white signs tacked up on rooms with four patients. Those that did not get it were out of luck to miss the vacation the rest of us got.

I would like to see the proofs of those pictures, the porcupines, too. I will send them back. I did not get the film for the cruise pictures yet. Half a dozen fellows have asked to borrow some of them. They all think I have a fine collection.

Dope says the 2 upper classes at the Point graduate this year. It has caused all kinds of discontent here. The one big topic of all rhino meetings now is how to resign and get in some outfit where you can see something a little more thrilling and dangerous than calc books. At the rate they are going now they will clean up the Germans before we graduate.

I could not go to Mass today as the place is still quarantined. I am nearly out of stamps.

Dan

OCTOBER 13, 1918

Dear Papa,

I am sorry to hear that John has been laid up. How long will it be before he can get around again? I read somewhere that the health department expected an epidemic of flu this winter to kill 15,000. We have heard that they are having a bad time with it up at the Lakes now. It is practically over here. We are still in quarantine and have no liberty, hops, nor football games. We do not get out to Mass on Sunday either. The place is absolutely dead. There is nothing to look forward to at the end of the week and the only thing to put any interest in Saturday and Sunday is the increased number of rhino meetings.

I had a rotten week in academic work. I would guess my marks to be: English 3.0, Math 3.0, Dago 3.0, Skinny 2.9, Mech 3.4. I was not as well fixed in Skinny as I thought when I returned to duty. All week I have been putting in about two hours a day on it so I am pretty nearly up to date now. A trip to the hospital is almost certain to knock a fellow's marks down for a week at least.

Sir Eric Geddes reviewed the healthy remnant of the regiment last Thursday. The place was infested with movie camera men and they say the review was fine so you may be able to see some pictures of the bunch in action.

The films arrived last night. There is a waiting list of fellows who want to borrow them.

Have you ordered the Naval Institute? I am allowed to get a membership on requisition and if you have not already subscribed I think I will do it. It is easily the best magazine on naval affairs.

I shipped a suitcase full of my old books home this morning. I have $44 amount available. As far as I can dope out the entire amount credited to me counting reserved pay, liberty bond, and mess entrance fee is $264.

Dan

OCTOBER 20 1918

Dear Papa,

Last week was a black one in the history of the Academy. To all present indications hazing, running, class rates, and all old time honored unofficial customs and traditions have been knocked off. A number of the 4th classmen who did not have the "guts" to stand up and take the gaff as the rest of us have all done wrote home and complained that they were being brutally hazed and maltreated. Some men sent home lists of names of those who hazed or ran them. These letters were sent to the

Supe and SecNav and they came down on us like the wrath of heaven. There have been threatened hazing investigations all week. There is not a man here with a stripe on his arm who has not hazed and when we found out what squealers we were up against not one of us felt safe.

We got an awful cussing out from the Com and our Batt officer told us that the only course left was to knock off rates entirely. He admitted when he was telling us to knock off that in his opinion hazing as practiced here was a fine thing for the plebes but his orders to knock it off came from higher up. I know I am mighty thankful for every bit of hazing I got last year. A lot of it was not a bit pleasant either.

Personally I think that rating plebe, being hazed and run, and being forced to abide by unofficial class rates do more to make a raw young cit into a responsible officer than anything else we have here. It certainly develops a deference for rank and a respect for custom and tradition. Most of the physical hazing a fellow gets comes from busting rates or not knowing something which tradition says he should know. Another thing that rating plebe does for a fellow is to reduce his idea of his own importance.

Now a youngster cannot even tell a plebe to brace up without exposing himself to the danger of going down for hazing. Now if a plebe feels like it he can carry on at the table all the time. Last year we used to carry on only when the Navy won a football game. Last year when we were not boning for the academic department, we were boning seamanship or learning the ships and admirals of the fleet for some youngster. Now the plebes bone the Cosmo or the RedBook. Some of the plebes that have some sense and know a good thing when they see it are rating plebe voluntarily now that we are unable to make them rate it. I would consider it a great misfortune if I had gone through here without rating plebe and being run and hazed.

As for the fellows who are taking advantage of this and not rating plebe, they are out of luck. There are 300 fourth classmen on the pap every morning since the reformation. We do not honor them with the name of plebe anymore. They are the gentlemen of the fourth class. Next year they will not rate youngsters unofficially.

I guess my week's marks as: Math 3.4, Dago 3.0, Mech 3.2, Skinny 3.2, English 3.0. I weigh only 125 with my gym outfit on. I am working out every night and am out for 129 wrestling so I hope to put on some beef before long.

Dan.

NOVEMBER 3 1918

Dear Papa,

. . . I was on duty yesterday so I missed liberty, the game and the hop.

'21 at the Point graduated a few days ago and now rate salutes from us besides having a good chance to see some action. There is dope now about going back to the old four year course. If the war is over I hope they do shift. It would be a great life here in peace times. There is also dope about the first class graduating in February.

There will be no hazing investigation. If they had one there is no telling where the axe would fall. There is not a man in the first or youngster class who has not hazed frequently. It was done as a matter of routine and no thought whatever was given to it. It is entirely knocked off now though. The freshman (they aren't plebes anymore) are now living by the reg book and that is the way they will live next year. They won't rate youngsters as my class rates now.

Did you have those films I took at Great Lakes during leave developed yet? There were four pictures of Ralph, John and Tom Collins, and myself. If you have I would like to have copies of them.

I went to Holy Communion today.

Dan

DECEMBER 22, 1918

Dear Papa,

Merry Christmas! The enclosed marks are not much of a Christmas present so I am sending "The Fighting Fleets" by Paine, too. Paine has actually been on destroyers during arguments with the subs so it ought to give a pretty good story of the life over there.

I was agreeably surprised with my math and steam marks. If I can hold the pace in those and get back to normal in English again I ought to break some of my records this month.

I had a scrap last week. Young Daniels put in his resignation and I called him a draft dodger. That was a week ago. He wanted to go out behind the gunshed then and there and settle it with our fists. That is a bouncing offence if you are ragged so I told him I would settle it in the gym with gloves. That is the usual way to settle scraps around here but that did not suit him. He said that the day his resignation was accepted and he shoved off that he would come up to my room and knock the stuffing out of me. He is 20 years old and has about 15 pounds on me. His resignation was accepted Friday and he came around that afternoon. Carl and I cleared the room for action and then Carl stood watch outside while Daniels and I had it out. I knocked him out in five minutes and when he came back to earth he said he was satisfied and had enough. He did not want to shake at first but he did before he left. I have no visible signs of the battle while he will have a beautiful shiner to explain to the Secretary.

There is no danger of any trouble over the affair as Daniels said it was closed as far as he was concerned and I think he is man enough to stand by it. He was a cit when the battle took place so I don't see how anything can happen.

I wish I could be home and have a real Christmas and see the tree again. Carl and I are going to decorate the room but it won't come anywhere near being a real Christmas. I hope everyone at home enjoys the day.

Dan.

DECEMBER 29, 1918

Dear Papa,

I got a nice scare last week. I was called down to see the Com and of course knew right away what it was about. I had to wait for half an hour and while waiting I had imagined every kind of a fate from hanging to life in the brig. When I was called in he asked me for the straight dope on the scrap, confidentially, and after I told him enough about it to bilge a regiment he told me that my conduct was entirely blameless. This coming from the Commandant personally means that I have nothing to worry about.

I don't believe the Secretary would try to make things uncomfortable. He could not bounce me without walking right into the accusation that he did it for personal reasons.

All the big papers here had stories of about half a column on the affair. They all had the same wrong dope the Trib had. The New York Herald was the only paper giving the straight story. It had half a column on the fourth page and said a youngster cleaned up Daniels. A Boston and an Indiana paper had no editorials on the wrong side. The class president is having the straight dope written up for the Associated Press now that the Com has said it was o.k.

Toward the beginning of the year I gave Daniels a workout which would have been nothing but a matter of course for a real plebe. He however was highly indignant at my impudence in hazing the Secretary of the Navy's son. On that account he has had it in for me all along. The fact that he had 20 pounds on me and a rep as a boxer which I have not also made him anxious for the fight. Two other fellows who called him a draft dodger got down on their knees to him when he looked cross about it.

There were no eye witnesses to the scrap. Koops helped us clear for action and then stood guard at the end of the corridor while the battle was in progress. There were no interruptions as rough houses are not uncommon and no one pays attention to a little racket.

I got myself in solid with the class by the affair. Quite a number of fellows that I never knew before say howdy when we meet now. It was also the scandal of Crabtown for several days and I got acquainted with several femmes on account of it.

I gave the Com the straight account of the affair. I even told him that I had hazed Daniels and exactly what I had said to him. He seemed amused at my opinions about his resigning and I think admitting I had hazed him without any sparring around made a good impression on him. It certainly was a great relief when he said the matter was o.k. . . .

I had a stroke of hard luck last week and collected 25 demerits at one fell swoop. I was section leader in Skinny and in calling the roll I thought I heard one man answer to his name when he was in reality absent. I reported him present and then the prof discovered he was not there and stuck me down for "ordinary neglect of duty." The batt officer has been raving lately about skipping formations and changed the report to "important neglect of duty" and plastered me 25 demerits. It was all a pure bust on my part and there was no intention at all of getting away with anything but that did not help matters.

I went to 10 o clock Mass today so I am writing Sunday night. It is the second time I have missed early Mass this year. I went to Holy Communion Christmas.

Happy New Year

Dan.

OCTOBER 12 1919

Dear Papa,

. . . We had a big upheaval here last week but it was all due to some feather brained idiot on the Baltimore Sun. There were two plebes in this last batt who wanted to resign. Their parents would not let them. Both of them got gloomy and morose over it and one of them stabbed himself and the other drank iodine. All the plebes that knew them say they were both known as "queer" ever since they came in. Both will recover and both deny emphatically that hazing had anything to do with their actions. They were just sick of the place . . . and both of them were weak minded anyhow. Some newspapers openly stated that they had been ordered to commit suicide by upperclassmen and accused us of being murderers and cutthroats. We might have been murderers if we could have got hold of the guy that wrote that article. A damned fool on a newspaper can do a lot of harm.

It is a reflection on the intelligence of the general public the way that story was believed. There was a resolution introduced in Congress to have a hazing investigation here. I wish it had gone through. An investigation would have cleared the place of all the charges the papers made.

Letters came from all over the country from people who fell for the line of bull in the papers. Most of them were so abusive and insulting that the writers were too yellow to sign their names to them.

The funny part of the whole thing is that there has been less running this year than ever before. There has been practically no hazing i.e. physical workouts and absolutely none of this brutal stuff the newspapers talk about. The plebes this year are being treated like kings compared to the way we were plebes year. Last week the Com told us that we would have to knock off what little hazing was going on when the press howl started. When the plebes in my company heard of it they voluntarily and on their own initiative got up a petition signed by all the plebes in the company to have the old rates and customs continued and said they did not want to have running knocked off.

Most of us were not scared by the prospect of an investigation but we were all raving mad at those newspapers for the lies they printed. I could go before the Supe right now and tell him everything I have done to plebes since I came back and he could not find a thing to object to. . . .

I went to Holy Communion this morning.

Dan.

JANUARY 25 1920

Dear Papa,

I think you put things a little too strong in that last letter. I'll admit I rated being bawled out but you said several things I don't agree with. You said I had violated my word of honor and cannot be trusted. As you say a naval officer's honor is his most valued possession and still is mine. When I said last September that I intended to star I was merely stating my honest intentions and did not intend to make any promises. On the other occasions when I said the same thing I did not intend it to be taken as a promise but merely as a statement of my intentions. That I have not starred is my own fault but it does not mean I lied when I said I intended to. You also said that I am a bum and that a bum is a person completely lacking in all principles of manhood. If I were such a character I would not have lasted 2½ years here. I have been lazy as far as studies are concerned but no one can say I have been a bum in other respects. I may be a damned fool for letting my opportunities slide by but a damned fool can have a lot of manhood in him. . . .

There seems to be another hazing mess in the offing. As far as I can see there is no occasion for it. Some plebes who are bilging did not have the guts to tell them at home that they bilged through their own laziness or woodenness and wrote home blaming it on hazing. I think it will blow over but if it doesn't it won't bother me. I haven't done any hazing and there has been almost none whatever since last October.

I was initiated into the first and second degrees of the Knights of Columbus last night. It was pretty good. I take the third Feb. 21. All those on the inside tell me that will be a lot better. There were about 70 other midshipmen initiated at the same time. After it was over several of us were called on for short speeches and I was one of the victims. They got everything straight about my belonging to the Chicago Council.

Our first wrestling meet is next Saturday but it will only be the second string men that get in. Another fellow and I have to wrestle it out for our weight Tuesday and the loser goes in, the winner being considered the first string man. I think I will lick him. There were three of us tied for the position last week but we busted the other one up and he won't be back for three weeks. I was handled roughly a week ago but I am o.k. now except for a sprained thumb which don't bother me much.

I went to Holy Communion today.

Dan.

CHAPTER 10

Love to All

The Letters of Charles John Weschler

Charles Weschler died as a Japanese prisoner of war on 6 January 1945, leaving behind a young wife and a little daughter. His younger sister, Sister Mary Charles Weschler of the Sisters of Mercy, knows well the events leading up to her brother's death. In a letter written years later, Sister Mary Charles explained that Charles had been on "Corregidor, but was being sent to Australia because he was a naval architect. The plane carrying him was forced down on Mindanao. Some of the passengers were picked up by another plane. Charles was among those who tried to repair the first plane, but before they could do so, the Japanese took them prisoner. He was in Davao and Bilibid prisons. In late 1944 or 1945, he and hundreds of other Americans were put in the holds of Japanese ships carrying Japanese personnel back to Japan. These ships were bombarded by American planes. He escaped from the first ship that was bombed but was recaptured; wounded in the second bombing; put on a third ship and died at sea January."

Certainly Midshipman Weschler had no idea of his fate when he wrote home from the academy. His letters brim with affection for the institution and for his family. He writes about dances, Army–Navy preparations, graduation. This correspondence provides a window into the spirit of a young man, a U.S. Naval Academy graduate, who sacrificed everything for his country.

AUGUST 12 1928 SUNDAY 6:40 A.M.

Dear Dad,

We're the Navy sugar babies this morning—no church party this morning because the first classman in charge didn't care to go out in the rain. At least that [is] what it will look like to the people of St. Mary's

Charles John Weschler
Courtesy The Lucky Bag/*USNA Nimitz Special Collections*

Church this morning when we fail to put in an appearance. The real reason is that a 75 mile gale is driving one of the heaviest rains I've ever seen; if we went to church in that at the end of our 15 minute walk we would be drowned; walking, of course, is our only way of getting there.

10:30 A.M.

Well we went to church anyway in all that rain; despite the fact that we wore mackintoshes and rubbers, I was soaking wet from my hips down. This is actually the worst rain storm I've ever seen; it has been teeming rain ever since yesterday morning and driven by a constantly rising wind. This morning we woke up to find the floor of our room soaking wet; and the windows open only 3 inches at that. The sailboats tied up to the dock are all sunk and will be out of commission about 2 weeks. Trees are down all over in Annapolis and the streets are all flooded. Just to be cheerful, Philburn tells us that the wind blows like this all winter.

But don't think the weather has dampened my spirits in the least; in fact, ever since yesterday morning I've actually been strutting because I was so pleased with myself and my good fortune. Yesterday morning we began a new drill at infantry practice (the first drill in which I've been on equal basis with everyone else); it's called "butts manuel"—or exercise under arms. It's done to music—quite familiar music too—just what you get over the radio in the morning about 7:00. Anyway I'm tickled pink because I caught on to the exercises immediately. Then yesterday noon I wore my white service; the coat is too large and will have to be altered; but the pants are just right. Boy, did it feel good to wear real pants with a belt instead of regular pajama pants with a draw-string.

After choir, on account of the rain, we had a gab fest in my room; and after a while settled down to a game of bridge. That afternoon was my first idea of the real fun a gang of fellows can have together at college; telling stories; pulling all kinds of pranks; and making merry in general. I guess we consumed about 3 lbs of fig bars during the course of the afternoon. We would have had pretzels only they were all gone Friday night. Last night in the pouring rain we went over to Mahan Hall (2 blocks away) to see Douglas Fairbanks in the "Goucho." We were all so wet when we got there we took our pants off and wrung them out before we sat down. The show itself was real good; add to that the wise cracks made by 55 middies and you can understand why we had a regular circus.

This morning too has been more or less of a side show ever since I woke up at 6 o clock to find papers floating around on the floor. Everybody seems as happy as a kid because he could get all wet and then put on dry clothes. Just now I'm wearing my white service trousers and my navy blue sweater (may it someday be enhanced with a big N—there are some 20 ways of getting a letter you know). Appetites are still good too; after a big dish of breakfast food, a dish of peaches, cocoa, and about a dozen flapjacks with maple syrup—I came to the room and between four of us ate another 1 pound of fig bars.

If anybody should ask you if I like this place tell them yes with a capital Y; and that I'm only beginning to catch the spirit; after the spirit gets me good I'll hate to leave the place, no doubt. I'm most satisfied. . . .

Well I think I've run out of material now so I'll say goodbye till Tuesday P.M. Love to everybody in the small family.

Charles

JANUARY 15 1929 TUESDAY EVENING

Dearest Mother and All,

Honestly Mother I don't know what to say about all this sickness going about, and the deaths of so many people. I know one thing, I have a mighty fervent prayer that no serious illness strikes the immediate family. Conditions around here are about the same as back home. We have over 100 fellows in the hospital with the flu—believe me I'm watching myself awfully close. It wouldn't be so tough to miss a few days now—but to start next term with a visit to the hospital would be mighty discouraging. May God be with all of us and keep us healthy.

I certainly was surprised to hear about Nancy Knoll. You could have pushed me over with a feather when I read your letter then when you told me Denney was home, I slumped—that shows how disconnected we are around here. Last Friday night I was over to his room and next day he shoves off for home. Who knows what will ever happen next? I recall so plainly the day I went up to Aunt Ida's to say good-bye before I left for the Naval Academy. She was still in bed with the baby. The little thing is already gone. I'd say that was a mighty tough break for the Knolls. Try to extend my sincere sympathy to them. I guess they'll understand how I feel about it. . . .

Well I must get back to work. You're right I'm getting settled down to the Naval Academy. It's not so bad. Treat your hand with care and tell everyone to keep well.

Love to all,
Charles

APRIL 21 1930 SUNDAY AFTERNOON

Dearest Mother and all,

All but an hour gone of my precious rest between watches. On account of a special party last evening my section had to stand duty until taps—then rise this morning before reveille, have an hour out for breakfast then on till dinner. And now at 3:30 I must go on again until 7:30. Thank goodness we can study for exams while on watch or I fear I should fall asleep on my feet. Aside from this watch, life is as sweet as ever.

Yesterday Navy came through splendidly in the track meet. I ran two miles but wasn't in striking distance of the winners. My time was 11 minutes 52 seconds for a distance equivalent to running from 116 West 21 Street to Prep and back again. That makes it sound good anyway. After the meet I did a bit of bumming around and dropped down to Mrs. Chestnut's. She had some home-made candy eggs for us all. When I arrived the plant we had sent her was already there. She appreciated it, just as we enjoy having her place to go to.

I, too, hope there will be a $7.50 excursion so you can come down. This time we can stop out there to talk. They are quite anxious to meet you, and I want you to know them.

Today is glorious—warm, sun-shining, tulip gardens blooming, everything a fresh spring green, not to forget that everyone has a suitable smiling countenance to go with the Easter finery that all their girl friends are sporting.

Easter sure is a great day. There was communion service at the chapel at 7 o clock this morning—almost half the regiment got up voluntarily to attend. It seems to be a day of universal goodness, kindness and happiness. "Alleluia" seems the right word to describe it.

There seems to be quite a few stories about the Navy just now. The American Magazine has two good ones in this issue; but that Guantanamo Blues in Liberty is just a lot of bad dope. The officers have taken special pains to tell us to ignore that.

Now I think before I go back on duty I shall try to grab me about forty winks—another Easter almost past. It will surely be pleasant to celebrate with the family again soon.

Good bye, mother dearest, hope you all had a happy Easter. I'm enjoying my box.

Love to all,
Charles

JUNE 2 1930 SUNDAY MORNING

Dearest Mother and All,

June Week is among us! What a style Parade, what a galaxy of color, what a variety of uniforms—Admirals, Major Generals, Colonels, Marines, Cadets, and Midshipmen! First class endangering the lives of pedestrians in their jubilation at being allowed to ride in machines. Second Classmen and Youngsters racing madly back to the Hall after their dates just exactly in time—some late. Plebes in seventh heaven showing off their Naval Academy to their O.A.O.'s yet just a little skittish about what shall happen on the cruise; and old grads, back for a reunion, visiting their old rooms and boasting about "When I was a midshipman."

Decoration Day—the guests have begun to arrive, the craning of necks, oh's and ah's at formation, all hands falling out of ranks to dine out with their folks or friends.

You know how my morning was spent—in exuberation over my successful year. In the afternoon Mitch and I went out to a show and then dropped in on one of our English Profs who has bachelor apartments. Mr. James is a great fellow—out of college only about four years and quite attached to the midshipmen. He has a wonderful collection of books, splendid music for his victrola and he's a mean hand on the mandolin and guitar. We were with him for almost three hours, laughing, talking, singing and eating. He sent us out to the kitchenette to make lemonade, while he called the grocer to send over supplies. It seems to be a great tradition in Annapolis that as soon as the midshipmen appear on the scene it means break out the chow. We do enjoy such hospitality.

In spite of the fact that it has been unusually chilly we went out on the roof in the evening to listen to the band concert, and afterwards I wandered over to Mrs. Chestnut's to see if the Knolls had come. They didn't arrive until 1:00 A.M. Saturday.

Saturday morning we had a bit of a drill and then prepared for the unveiling ceremony of Tecumseh. Everyone was here for that—class of 1891 en masse (they presented the statue), Secretary Adams, a flock of admirals, etc. Then while the ceremony was in progress the Los Angeles flew over. After about half an hour of speeches the veil was pulled aside and we were half hoping that Tecumseh would appear in his war paint—but the searchlight which had been turned on him all week did its work and he was just his modest self. And such a shower of pennies when the veil fell. Navy juniors made a mad scramble for this wanton display of wealth. . . .

And that ends my activities so far. First Class are now at chapel for Baccalaureate. We call it "sob" Sunday around here. And this afternoon we are expecting our girl friends. There will then be seven Erie girls on hand.

I think that's just about all the news I have so I will say good bye for a couple of days. While I am enjoying all this I cannot help but think what fun it will be two years from now when you are here to share the fun too.

Good bye, mother dearest.

loads of love,
Charles

JUNE 9 1930 SUNDAY MORNING

Dearest Mother and All,

Now to resume the narrative of events where I left off. Hope I can tell you all the news because there is quite a bit.

I finished the afternoon Parade which ended in a merry snake dance with all the first class who carried swords all year once more toting guns while Plebes carried their swords. First we had the best dinner ever at Carvel Hall, then to the dance. Such a crowd I never saw before and such color. The ball was decorated very tastily in blue, gold, and green. The reception platform and band stand were oases of roses and palms. Every midshipman, his O.A.O. and some friends were there. Dancing was next to impossible but who wants to dance at the June Ball when there is so much to see. Loretta and I kept our program faithfully till after the eighth dance, but dances were so short and the intervals so long that we gave that up. We went up on the balcony for a while to see the people. I can't describe the picture from there—such gorgeous gowns and so many varieties of uniforms. From there we strolled out to Smoke Park for refreshments.

That was another sight to behold. The beautiful park was illuminated with myriads of Japanese lanterns and a beautiful colored fountain in the center. There was starry sky above with a gorgeous moon while strains of classical music floated down from the terrace. We couldn't help but be impressed with the splendor of it all. Needless to say we spent a good part of the evening in these picturesque surroundings watching the people pass along. This part gave me the greatest thrill of June Week, in fact of all my time at the Naval Academy. I know Loretta was very much pleased and impressed. My next thrill shall be in showing you all this.

On our return from the hop we were too excited to sleep so we passed a good bit of our time gabbing and harassing the poor plebes for the last time. Formation next morning was a continuation of this spirit of carry on—instead of marching to breakfast we strolled down in mob formation. We left breakfast at will. What a rare treat this all was.

And then graduation. It is really a simple ceremony, yet it means so much. Parents waving to their sons seated before the platform, visitors and friends in every conceivable point and a bank of midshipmen in full dress on either side of the white clad graduates. Then after brief speeches the presentation of diplomas and lusty cheers from the midshipmen's stands as each company commander became an ensign and another batch of plebes became youngsters.

But the sight in the Yard afterward was more impressive. Plebes carrying on their traditional ceremony around Herndon monument while sweethearts and mothers with proudly beating hearts pinned the epaulets on the graduated to complete the uniform—then a fond embrace. We just strolled around the Yard witnessing episode after episode and filled with an indescribable feeling—so proud to be around to see it all.

In the afternoon we partook of the only mode of water travel the girls hadn't tried. We all went sailing and swimming all afternoon, victrola along to provide the music. It was really a fitting climax to the week. We no longer had to talk but simply sat around enjoying the water, the breezes and the sights from the water.

We kept our same party of six at the evening meal—Dan and Vee, Phil and Beverly, Loretta and I. We had a grand time over a leisurely meal and then returned to Mrs. Chestnut's for one half hour when our time with the girls was practically over. How we all hated to say goodbye. We tried to laugh it off. Finally, we left with the understanding that we would see the girls at seven thirty and go down to bid Dan bon voyage on the cruise. That again was a touching experience. The band was there playing spirited airs, the docks were crowded and everyone looked as if they were trying to hold back the clock. But the hour came and we waved good bye to all the boys. 32 was in charge at the Academy.

Now the girls had just twenty minutes till train time, and I was restricted to the Yard. We parted at Gate #2 quite reluctantly but with mutual expression of the grand time we had had.

The course of this letter, mother, has no doubt suggested many romantic moments, but you know that I didn't abuse your trust. I did nothing I wouldn't do before you. Loretta and I are the best of friends. I think the world of her, especially after this week. Her character is unimpeachable. I guess everyone had a better time than we expected.

Now the events of the last two days. Friday morning immediately after breakfast we got all our gear moved to the new room 2109 so that as soon as I said farewell to the girls I returned and began to square myself away. It was well that we were busy or lonesomeness might have overtaken us sooner. By noon we were flopped on our beds, surveying the view and cleanliness we had brought out of a chaos of two hours before hand.

At noon I assumed my duties as Mustering Petty Officer and already I feel quite familiar with my position. This morning I marched the Church Party thru town. I enjoy it. At three o clock we were granted liberty so we sallied forth thru #2 gate (our new possession) and took charge of Annapolis.

I stopped out in town to buy me the luxury of two silk undershirts and a handkerchief for my coat pocket. Then I met Shel and we stopped in to see Mrs. Chestnut for a few minutes. She was quite lonesome for all her guests. In the evening I planned to write but the newness of the surroundings, the memory of the past few days all tended to make us restless and unable to concentrate on anything. We simply wandered from room to room getting acquainted.

Yesterday it sure was fun to watch the boys leave for the weekend. Everyone perfectly dressed and carrying himself so proudly. They didn't have on their uniforms but they couldn't lose their carriage. I could pick them out wherever I went.

I'm quite glad that we didn't go out this first week because it has been sultry all the time, and I would so have hated to get my new clothes wet the first time I wear them. So far we have taken no pictures but we will soon.

This sure has been a lengthy discourse but I guess you can sort of follow my week pretty well. I hope that all of you manage to have a vacation this summer as pleasant as mine has been—really, it is only your cooperation that has made mine so happy and successful. I wish I knew how I could do something so that you might be able to say the same.

How this morning has flown by. Already it is time for dinner. I have been writing for fully two hours. I hope you are all well and happy. Soon school will be out for everyone and the holidays will be at hand. I'm wishing you all the happiest and healthiest summer you've ever had.

Good bye, mother dearest.

Loads and loads of love to all,
Charles

JULY 20 1930 SATURDAY AFTERNOON

Dearest Mother and All,

I'm sitting in my room dressed only in "skivvy" drawers, windows and doors open for a draft. Yes, I'm a bit comfortable but each breeze feels like it had just passed over a furnace first. Oh what I wouldn't give for some of those breezes out on a battleship. No thanks, tho, I don't care for that life.

Time sure has flown by this week, scarcely a minute to myself until this afternoon. I would say this week will be the most practical and valuable of the entire summer course. It has been our first training in being officers. I can take orders and interpret them properly. I can give commands in a military fashion and get obedience. I can be the hard-boiled top sergeant or I can be the kindly nurse to the new plebes, yet always keeping their full respect in as much as I am 2nd class and they are plebes. But the best part is that I can face an officer and carry on a conversation without a miss in my voice and quivering knees of yore. They are human after all. I can't exactly pass a verdict on myself but I feel quite confident that I know how to handle men. My hope now is that I get a chance first class year to prove myself.

Experiences all week have been novel but the climax came fittingly this noon when I was acting "five striper" of the plebes. This came not as a matter of merit but as one of routine. Little did I think 2 years ago as I stood in ranks as a quivering plebe that I now should be giving them the orders. Saturday noons there is always a "Skippers Inspection". That is the Commandant and all the officers make an inspection of the midshipmen. As commander of the Plebes I had to give all the commands to get them ready. It sure was funny to hear my voice echo and re echo between the wings of Bancroft Hall. I didn't realize my lungs were so strong. Everything went off very smoothly. Afterwards I was told that my work was well done. Compliments are so rare that I treasure it more dearly. In the mess hall then, instead of sitting with the midshipmen, I ate at the head of the Plebe staff table in the center of the mess hall. Chicas waiting on us hand and foot. One grand experience that being a "5 striper" for a day. Tomorrow I stand a lowly deck watch but at least I shall get rested up.

Wednesday evening I had a very pleasant diversion. Jane Snyder had a buffet supper for a party of ten couples. I was allowed to get off watch to attend. It was a farewell party for Polly (whom I met last Sunday) but it was also a birthday party for Jane. One trouble was that we had to leave at 9:30. I intend to keep up my acquaintance with Jane, you can bet.

There has been a great deal of excitement around here this past week. Last Sunday a couple of fellows brought two girls dressed in white works into the mess hall for evening meal. Somehow, they were found out and the trouble starts to brew. The girls were quite influential in Washington and pulled all strings to try to get the fellows let off easy. The fellows themselves rounded up congressmen from all over the U.S. Newspaper men have flocked around trying to get the news. About 12 girls in Washington claim to be the guilty ones. It has resulted in a lot of publicity, mostly unfavorable. The two guilty men have not yet heard their sentences. The man in charge of the table, a darn good boy who wouldn't think of cutting up, has lost his rank as a platoon commander and receives 75 demerits and 60 days on the ship, his September leave. The other 19 on the table are receiving 30 days on the ship and 50 demerits. A fine mess just for two fellows to stir up. They say they are doing this for disciplinary purposes but it strikes me as quite severe. I shall send you such clippings as I get from the newspapers.

The wind is blowing my paper away so I'll stop with more soon.

Good bye, mother dearest,
Love to all,
Charles

JULY 24 1930 THURSDAY AFTERNOON

Dearest Mother and All,

. . . I was about ready to do nothing over this coming weekend but when the letter came yesterday with a check from Dad I was no longer "stone broke". Once more I want to tell you all how much I appreciate all you have done to help make my summer my happiest time at the Naval Academy.

Our class are more or less a bunch of fools. They can't appreciate a good thing when they have it. All summer they have done nothing but impose on the allowances and privileges given. They put the wrong foot forward. At the start, we were given two week's probation but they didn't stop. The result has been a bearing down on the part of the executive department and Class A (seniors). Reports have been flying thick and fast. I don't say the fellows didn't rate them but it sure has made the discipline for all the rest of us more strict. So far this summer our class has accumulated over 6000 demerits, more than any class ever got in an entire year. The climax came with this affair of girls in the mess hall. Unfavorable publicity was the result in all the newspapers. But the anti-climax came in a letter published in last evening's Annapolis paper signed "two Midshipmen". They claimed to be expressing sentiments of the whole class and criticized the officials here at N.A. for the drastic action taken.

This morning the Admiral called representatives from each company to his office and explained to them that such action was a prison offence and cited Colonel Martin and Rear Admiral Magruder, both of whom were expelled from the service for such action. I fear very much that these two thoughtless eggs will be the cause of our losing the rest of our weekends. A class meeting will give us more dope. I shall keep you posted.

In reading over my past letter I find I overlooked mentioning Emory's mother's death. That sure was hard on him. While working with him he told me an awful lot about him. I know he thinks a lot of her. Ask Dad to please express my sympathy and say that I have said a prayer for her.

Almost time to "clear the decks" so I must say Good Bye.

Oodles of love to all, and you most, mother and dad,
Charles

NOVEMBER 14 1930 FRIDAY EVENING

Dearest Mother and All,

Hell has broken loose. That's the only way to describe it. Since noon today in the mess hall when they announced that there will be an Army Navy game on December 13 in New York, no one has been responsible for their actions. It was announced just before we sat down to table. The result was bedlam. Plates were broken, fellows pummeled each other like idiots; chairs were tossed back and forth; napkins waved, hats flew about and lungs were distorted. All during the meal we sang. Sang those grand, thrilling inspiring songs that hadn't resounded in Bancroft Hall for three years. Anchors Aweigh first verse was sung with meaning behind it. Army Mule was chanted and the battle cry was Beat Army.

After chow we all adjourned to Smoke Hall where "war was officially declared". We did powerful concentrated yelling and all hands shoved off to go to class knowing that we would play Army but not a thing about classes. Formations were but a formality and we all got them talking somehow about what we would do against Army and a night in New York.

By the time we returned from class everyone knew that they were kidding themselves about having a big night in Philly. We forego that bit of liberty with pleasure to wait a week to see the Army where Goat meets mule. Yells meet in the center of the field and blow up. Where blue and gold shall get mixed up with black and gray and gold.

Cheer practice started an hour ago. All hands were there en masse. We went over to the gym. Bill Ingram bawled us out for having our hammers out all season and advised us to get hot and stay hot from now until December 13th. All bygones are bygones. The team and the regiment are pals once more. We've an uphill fight ahead of us. Our team must play way over its heads to win, but we can do it. Bill was right in what he said so we took it between the eyes.

Just as we were about to break up, Admiral Robinson came into the gym to show some visitors around. Was he pleased to see us gathered together. He was happy as a kid, even danced a jig on the deck. I honestly think that he was more elated than any of us over having a game—if that is possible. He spoke encouragingly (not much was necessary) and we just about lifted the roof with a cheer for him.

Sad to say it's been raining all day so our exuberance had to stay penned up in the halls, so I have just returned, already quite hoarse and my ears ringing. And we're gonna beat the Army.

Gee, mother, I'm a plebe all over again. So are the rest of the underclass. Busy digging around, learning the old songs, finding out traditions, customs, rates! At last we've got that certain something of the Academy which has been lacking since I've been here. I can feel it already. A new pride in the service. A more secure binding together to bring about more fellowship. Something new has started. I hope we can all keep it going.

With this new attitude and fire among us I predict a victory tomorrow against SMU. We'll show Baltimore that it is possible for a Navy team to win in their town. We're off and there ain't no stoppin' us.

I expect I shall be requested to purchase tickets for various people but I find out the maximum number anyone can get is two. Guess diplomacy shall be necessary, especially if I decide to drag. . . .

Now perhaps I had better get ready for chow. I didn't realize it but I've been writing for a full hour.

Let's have all the news—and I'll keep you posted on our Army–Navy Game.

Good bye mother dearest,
Loads of love to all.
Charles

Beat Army!

CHAPTER II

Lucky Bag Holds the Stage

The Letters of Frank Kane Slason

The editor of the Naval Academy yearbook knew exactly what he wanted, as revealed in a letter to his family: "We've decided on the deep brown cover and will use modern photography and type with simple art work . . . modern type will be an innovation. I've been thinking about using eggshell finish paper. . . ."

Born in Staten Island, New York, Frank K. Slason took seriously his position as editor of the 1935 Lucky Bag. *With a business and organizational acumen that belied his years, Slason oversaw the creation of the yearbook. These letters discuss his budget concerns, his staffing problems, his heated discussions with printers and paper suppliers. The fellow enjoyed the power and activity of his position. As the 1935* Lucky Bag *neared completion, Slason worried "aloud" to his parents: "I'm really a bit afraid to finish the thing and be deprived of a lot of my activity. It may have a bad effect. You see, I'm used to driving things along no matter what happens. With the book finished I won't have anything upon which I can expend all that energy and I'm afraid I'll be rather lost for awhile until I can get used to having a lot of time to do a few things and become accustomed to the inactivity. . . ."*

Although Slason had civilian job offers before graduation, he chose to make the navy his career. He retired in 1959 as a captain and died in 1967.

7/27/31 8:15 PM

Dear Mother, Dad, and Joan,

In my room at last and finished for the day—and what a day! The physicals were brutally hard—took close to three hours—then we ate—

(good food, lots of it)—and after dinner we went down and drew our outfits—three big bags of stuff heavy as anything—consequently three trips from Midshipmen Store to room. Then to sort it (I haven't finished yet)—and get it numbered with one's laundry number.

I got a hair cut—in fact I got em all cut—all the boys do—for the summer I guess and it surely is plenty short—only about an inch long on the top of my head but you'd be surprised how good it looks when you get into your white works—they look exactly like pajamas—I drew my cap, that is, my dress cap—it's a nifty and a lot of other stuff—this writing paper along with everything else—I don't know just when I'll send home my clothes—very shortly anyway.

Tomorrow I'm going out for crew—at 4:30—and now I'm going to make up my bed and get into it soon—according to my regulations book, taps are at 10:00 and I'd like to drop Betty Yater a line on this paper—now ask me why.

The place here is grand—nothing better, and all the fellows are awfully nice—they drop around at your room and talk—in fact it seems that everyone seems to know everyone else.

My roommate for the present (we pick our own later) is an awfully nice little fellow from Cuba—he's as funny as a hedge fence and has been down here for quite a little while—consequently he shows me just how things are to be folded and put away.

Drop me a line or two at the following address and keep the form—it must be exact to the letter:

Midshipman Frank Kane Slason
United States Naval Academy
Room 3126
Annapolis Maryland

I have quite a bit of cash left over and am doubtful as to what to do with it. You tell me.

I think it might be a good idea if I started a schedule for writing and adhere to it rigidly—but that can take care of itself—at any rate, however, my letters will all be numbered—the number before the date, consequently if the letters you receive do not have their numbers in sequence

Frank Kane Slason
Courtesy The Lucky Bag / *USNA Nimitz Special Collections*

you'll know that one or two must be lost—this letter is number one—the number before the date.

I'm gonna close now family and say goodnight—I'm sure plenty tired—I'll write again very very soon.

Lots and lots of love for all
Frank

2—7/28/31
Dear Mother, Dad, and Joan,

I can sit down and really write a letter because I've stencilled all of my equipment and have it mostly stowed away—I have tomorrow (all day) to get it finished—then Thursday I attend all formations. I haven't found it so hard—and am learning fast—and honestly, when you really consider the way (that is, discipline, salutes and order) that they require is really the simplest—incidentally you should see the snappy salute I can give—

As I've already told you, I've drawn all my clothes and you would be positively aghast at the pile of stuff I have, a classy raincoat with a cape, a nifty cap with a gold anchor on the front—and by the way, I was measured for my winter service.

The food we get is positively grand (sorta heavenly) and you should see all we get—I drink seven or eight glasses of milk a meal—plus all the other food—incidentally, Mother, the cooking is very very very much like yours; good, healthy, substantial solid food. It makes good eating and it's no wonder we put on weight.

The beds are good too—nice and comfortable, and the way we have to make them up keeps the covers (nice square folded corners, Mister) tucked in around all night.

I sent the bag and all my civilian clothes home today. Y'see the reason why I sent the bag is this: they store them in the cellar—which wouldn't do them any good after five months and when I do come home for Christmas—if I want to bring much of my own clothes (Regulation, I mean) I can have you send the bag. It's cheaper than the depreciation; 'course too, I'll wear "cits" most of the time during the Christmas season.

I have twenty five dollars here that I cannot use. Now if you want me to shoot it home just let me know and I'll send you a money order for it. I'll have no use for it other than to buy a stamp or two—stamps are the only things you can't draw on your $9.00 a month, but you can draw anything, or things, up to $9.00 in a month and the balance carries over into the next month. So I won't need much cash.

Do write and keep me informed about Dinkle—I'd like to know.

Now if you'll 'scuse me till the next time I'll close and get off a few lines to Betty Yater—she doesn't know yet—I wrote a telegram—it came back—it's in the flannels in the bag I sent home.

I'll write again tomorrow (I'll post this tomorrow and tomorrow's the next day) so until then, night night with

Loads of love for everyone (aunts)
Midshipman Frank

P.s. Tell the Aunts I'll write soon—I'm terribly rushed.

5—8/1/31
Dear dear Mother—

I just got your letter after coming down from being inoculated and vaccinated and am sitting right down to write and (that is, answer it)—as for the inoculations and vaccinations—it is required of the fourth class—it didn't hurt a bit and I feel fine as the fact that I can sit right down and write a letter will testify. As for that money I have, as long as it's not necessary for me to send it back, I'll keep it—cause there are some uses for cash here and we only get two dollars a month—some things at the midshipmen store are bought for cash only and other things may be taken out of your $9.00 requisition for a month—that's credit only and cannot be drawn as cash. This writing paper by the way is quite cheap—only fifty cents a box—(large box too) so the idea that I can write to you on cheap paper is all wet—you'll get the best paper I've got—I got the letter from Edy and the two or three you sent—they arrived in the middle of the week—as for writing Hal—well he'll have to wait till I get a little time—maybe this evening—I sent a letter to the Aunts—I did want to get it off sooner but didn't have a chance—you'll let me know about Dinkle—as for feeling that I'm compelled to write to you—you get the queerest ideas—why I don't feel that it is compulsory—I do it cause I honestly want to write and tell you about things—why it's just like talking to you, only it's on paper—I'll write every chance I get—as I have been doing—and listen here Mrs. S if I had two letters to write, one to you and one to some outsider, who do you suppose I'd write to—why it's almost ridiculous to even think that any letter takes precedence over yours.

Tell Jerry thanks an awful lot for cleaning the garage—and that I'll probably write him tonight—y'see they have movies at Mahan Hall and as we were inoculated we are required to stay in our rooms.

By the way Momsey (I meant to tell you this before but I forgot), when my teeth were being examined on the physicals they had to be exrayed to see if the extractions were clean ones and of course some of the filled teeth were exrayed too—the dental corps got around my chair and together with the exrays and my teeth, were admiring Dr. Walsh's work. You tell him about it when you and Joan go down again. I know about the dinner party so [it's] probably best that you don't write—you'll be pretty busy—incidentally I've gotten quite a few letters—one from Hap, one from Doc, and several from you as well as the one from Edy (the one you sent) I'm expecting one from her anyday now—perhaps in the afternoon mail—Y'know I've just been looking out my window at the Terrace, and the trees and Dahlgren Hall—all covered with the greenest ivy and it's dawned on me that although I've only been here a week I'm crazy about the place already. Dahlgren Hall is the Armory where they have the Infantry rifles and bayonets and at each end they have four of the most beautiful five inch guns you've ever seen—also some "swell" anti-aircrafts. As for food, well it's certainly good that the government is feeding me considering the way I'm eating—pretty nearly a quart of milk a meal (3 to 5 glasses) and several helpings of everything else; and we sure get great food—steaks, chicken, roast beef, every meal—except of course breakfast. I'm going to close now m'honey and get dressed for another grand and glorious meal so I'll say so long with all the love in the World multiplied by 100000 from

Frank

P.S. When you write my name you can just put a K for Kane—as long as it has all the initials, it's ok.

5 8/5/31

Dear Mother, Dad, and Joan,

I'm not quite sure whether this letter is five or six—at any rate it's a letter so the number doesn't matter. We have just finished having inspection and must stay in our rooms for quite a while so I've decided to write and tell you about this morning—We went over to rifle range and I had my first tussles with Miss Springfield—boy those guns sure have a kick but firing them is great fun because they are so exact. I qualified prone slow fire, sitting slow fire, and rapid fire prone. I was firing for three hours steadily. Enclosed is a little souvenir of my work on the range—one of the shells we use—it's fired and is one of the shells I made a bulls eye with—the range is two hundred yards and of the three ways of firing, rapid is the hardest—one lies down and fires ten shots in sixty seconds. It's not so hard to fire but it's the pounding that's disconcerting. I made a 46 out of a possible fifty in rapid, and boy my shoulder is sore yet. It's lots of fun tho' and I'm looking forward to my next time on the range. I'm still out for crew and expect to get into a shell today as we have one hour and a half recreation period, no, we have two and a half hours. I got Hal's letter but don't know whether I'll be able to answer it before Sunday. I drew my first pay today—two dollars—which is our pay for a month—I don't know how I got a month's pay but I did, so I'm not kicking—at two dollars a month one would have twenty four dollars in a year—it's all clear profit too because there's no way under the sun to spend it—y'see we only go outside the grounds on Sunday and then are marched (the Catholics) to the Catholic church and back. Of course, we can requisition $9.00 worth of stuff at the store a month so the two bucks are almost clear profit. This afternoon, as I said before, we have recreation so I'm going over to crew. By the way Dad, I got your letter and it's one of the best I've gotten since I've come here—nice and long. You'd be surprised how nice a long letter is here—it's so easy for people outside to write long letters but it's awfully hard to write a long letter from here to outside—y'see everything is so much the same here that it's awfully hard to say anything—of course lots of things happen that are interesting in here but would be awfully flat for you to read. Incidentally, I took my strength tests and expect I flunked 'em. Y'see I'm so tall that they expect a very very strong person which I am not—anyway they give you another and another chance and finally nobody stays home from Christmas leave on account of those—so don't worry. I'll write again on Saturday family—and so until then I'll say toodle oomps with all the love in the woild from

Skipper

SUNDAY 22 OCTOBER 1933

Dear Mother and Dad and Joan—

Howdy, howdy—back again after a week of absence and a week of much done, mostly checked up to profit—no debits as yet. I got Joan's and Dad's letters together last Tuesday and yours came on Friday Mother. As a whole the week was good but I don't quite know where to start. I got a lot done on the L.B., Log, Trident and Ring Committee (also Reception Committee) but the L.B. holds the stage at present. Norm and I have been threshing out things and have about decided on the general tenor of the book. My typewriter has been humming; and I've gotten out plenty of letters getting information about paper, type, methods of printing. I think the book, if we work it as we'd like to, will be "slick". We've decided on the deep brown cover and will use modern photography and type with simple art work (where we use it)—very little art work, as it's generally not 100% perfect and costs plenty. Photography, with trick lighting effects, can do more, and do it cheaper too, than any art work I've yet to see. Modern type will be an innovation. I've been thinking about using eggshell finish paper—like this that I'm writing on but find that the ordinary half to me won't print on it. I've been writing here and there getting dope on offset lithography. If we go as we want to the following things will be new to Lucky Bag: 1) Modern Type 2) Eggshell paper 3) no art work 4) offset lithography. Some half dozen letters trying to get dope on the four little new things caused a bombshell among the conventional L.B. contractors. DeJonge can't handle eggshell paper (a three page letter from DeJonge showing signs of panic follows); J&O specialize (more or less in artwork)—they sob and cry and say that sort of art work is the keynote of an annual. DuBois can't print it offset—he's coming down for an all afternoon conference from Rochester today. . . . We'll get something out of these people, by golly.

Sunday night—Was out to dinner at Carvel today seeing a Mr. Sullivan of DuBois printing in cooperation with the Bureau of Engraving. They've crystallized our ideas as to the book and after a three hour threshing about we've been more or less committed to a certain book. We have some sample page layouts already. We'll go all through the thing with action photography—modern type—simple, modern, but not modernistic art work in a few cases but as a whole our division pages will be about $150 cheaper as well as being much more beautiful than any other books. Its simplicity gives it beauty and class. It's going to be modern, new, active, and will tell you better than anything you ever saw of Academy life—life of '35 in particular. I could go through the entire book for you right now. I'm awfully enthusiastic about it—can't wait to get going—to get things done. If we put it together as we planned to-day, and there's no reason why we shouldn't, I wouldn't be a bit surprised to see two editions go through the press. Everyone will be interested because though it's our book there's a chance to find one's picture on any page. Take for instance the pictures of the stripers under "administration"—instead of taking them sitting primly in chairs we'll take 'em marching—marching in a staff formation—the camera placed nearly on the ground—or shots from directly in front and above—different, every single one of them—action in every single one of them. But in the final analysis every single person showing as everyone is used to seeing him—relaxation is what these books need—relaxation and some of this half rate art work removed. It's something you dream about but never expect to see—as yet, my enthusiasm is based upon ideas—as light as the morning mist—but patience yet awhile and you'll have something by which you may judge my pep and energy. At least we have something to expend our efforts on—something to do—and it's worthwhile—You can't imagine how nice it is to have something to really "put out" for—and be able to. . . .

All for now peop. I have to study some electricity as have an exam in it tomorrow. Speaking of exams, I think I got a 3.90 in the Bull Exam.

Much love for all
Frank

POSTMARK 2/26/34

Dear Mother and Dad and Joan:

Another week gone by with not a lot to tell you about. I'm typing this because I'm down in the office and have nothing to do for the moment, so thought that I'd get at the weekly letter and try to give you a little dope about what has gone on here.

First off I came out of the hospital when I said I would and am quite in the best of health and spirits at present. It wasn't a bad cold though I did run a slight temperature for a day or so. I didn't miss any exams and think I made out pretty well on them all. I know I passed everything and am quite sure of having a lot of velvet in most everything but Nav this month. The Nav isn't so good because the exam was very tough and I only have a maximum 3.0 on it, due to the omission of the second problem thru lack of time. They may raise the grades of the entire class though and then I could get a bit over a 3.0 provided I had everything correct. I feel sure I passed it though and will not have to worry about anything. I may stand very high in Ordnance and Steam as I got daily grades and am quite sure that I got high marks on the two exams. No grades have been posted as yet but I will send them on as soon as they come up.

Have written to Grady but find that it is very hard to get people to write to him every day. I expect that they will all write but the idea of picking a day to do it doesn't sit well with most of them. I wrote last week and am writing as often as I can but find that I cannot write during the week.

L.B. coming along better than ever and I am amazed at the cooperation that I am getting from the staff in general and in several specific cases in particular. Bert Harden, an Associate Ed. is a ten strike. He comes down every day and has done reams of work. Everyone is interested and I find it hard to give them all enough work to do. It is a very comforting feeling to know that I can get all the cooperation that I want and actually have to keep people from doing too much. It leaves me plenty of time to hit it off on layouts for pages and I can now see that it will be an easy matter for me to design the entire book. A lot of layouts went to the Bureau (our engravers) a week or so ago and we will be getting the finished things back soon, so we can see how they will look when they are printed. I design the layout and make up the specifications and the Bureau makes it up with pictures on it and puts in the color. We can see how it will look in the finished book. It will be quite a thing to be able to say that I designed an entire 525 page book right down to the placing of the type and in some cases the setup for the particular pictures.

Am awfully pleased to hear the Kid Sis is boning her pretty head off so to speak. . . . does she still do any drawing?

Speaking of drawing reminds me that I'm going to do up an ad for the Navy Mutual Aid Advertising contest and try to win the $50. It's well worth the little time that I will put on it and it may be that I'll be the only one to put in an ad.

I was surprised that you thought I might not be able to handle the Log as well as the Lucky Bag. I intend to take it if I get the chance because it is something that I would be very foolish to let go by. I may just as well train myself to handle any amount of work that I decide. After all, what do I do? . . . mighty little when it comes right down to it. I waste a lot of time as it is as far as I can see. I may not be able to sweep with a broom but I'm pleased to think there is no job or jobs too big for me to handle. Between you and me if I had a chance for the Trident too I'd take it. It's snowing here again today and is very cold. There has been ice on the river and bay now for a long while and it seems sometimes as if winter was to be with us forever. This idea "if winter comes can spring be far behind" is all wrong. Spring can be very far behind and very often is.

Got the cullud paper and was joyful . . . used it to get some Bicarb so we can have hot Bicarbs when we get a cold. All the fancy stuff they had in the Hospital didn't do any good but as soon as I tried some hot Bicarb everything came under control. Will send back cullud paper the first of the month when my debtors crash through.

All for now people. I think I'll go over to the gym for a little while and try a few high jumps. Going out for track this spring y'know.

Much love to all,
Frank

P.S. Don't mind the typographical errors—haven't had a chance to proofread.

POSTMARK 3/12/34 SUNDAY NIGHT 9:55 PM

Dear Mother and Dad and Joan,

I have been as busy as the proverbial bee this weekend so have no time to write at length. Just want you to know if I'm alright, which I am, and that I have been doing much. Some layouts came back in smooth form today and I'm awfully pleased—if everything else goes as well I should have a book to be proud of when it's finished. Later in the afternoon I drew up a program cover for the Musical Club's performance and worked on my ads—cleared up three pages typed copy on the Log and had time to get off a letter to the Bureau. So I'm quite pleased with the weekend but wish I'd had more time to write. Next week, however, I'm on watch Saturday and will write a long letter then and tell you all about everything and answer your letters of the past week. . . .

Be good family—and I'll try to be

Much love to all

Frank

POSTMARK 3/20/34

Dear Mother and Dad and Joan

The past week has been one of detail work. Nothing big done and nothing sensational to write you about. We finished up the dummy and have a final count of 532 pages which will cost us some $18,250 to engrave, print and bind. That, with an income of $21,000 coming in, which gives us more than a ten percent margin in safety. A funny part of our estimates came about when I figured the cost of the engravings per page. I guessed at $15.00 and it came out to be $14.92—missed it by eight cents for an estimate of over 270 pages.

I've been quite discouraged this week in connection with the L.B. though. We gave the class a three week deadline in which each man was to write his room [mate's] biography—112 words. Only some thirty out of 160 came in in this Batt and heaven only knows what results in the other Batts were like. It was, all in all, a splendid demonstration of what cooperation should not be like. Worst of it all, I can't appear discouraged to the staff or anyone else because enthusiasm must be kept up. We can't force people to write 112 words because it might hurt circulation. In short, there isn't anything to do but sit back and trust that the fates will be kind. If results continue to be poor we'll take four days next week and have battalion meetings in which we'll try to convince the class that there's a reason for having their Biogs in early. And there is a reason. Our $18,250 figure is contingent upon our getting 60% of our engravings in on a 30% discount figure. Here a staff can work for two years and put out 532 pages but each man in the class can't write a little more than a hundred words in three weeks. This is the first big snag that we've hit and you can take my word for it that it's a sticker. It does me good to write and talk about it to you because I can't say anything about it here except encourage, cajole and appear that everything is going along in the pink. Actually, the situation is exceptionally serious due to the construction of our Biog page with references to the informal pictures—it's too long an explanation to give here but all those engravings and the way they're made depends upon Biographies—it'll all come out all right tho'. You mark my words. . . .

All for this time—be good people and keep well and happy.

Much love to all

Frank

OCTOBER 1934

Mother dear

Just a line to tell you that I got down here all right and am in the swing of things already—was quite easy getting acclimated. This is only a note to tell you that and to ask that you do something for me.

When I left I forgot one very important thing. It is some matter pertaining to the letting of contracts that are of the utmost delicacy. What I want you to do is this: Go up to my closet and on the shelf over the boxes and under that little chinese box Lefty gave me is that brown leather wallet. Take it just as it is, being careful not to open it, as the order of things must not be disturbed and wrap it and send it on as soon as possible. It is very important that you do just as I have outlined because I have a carbon copy of this letter and I want to be absolutely certain that I can authenticate anything written here. Just take it down, put several elastics around it so that it will stay tightly shut, wrap and send first class mail. Remember it is very urgent that it must not be opened—be sure that it stay as shut—I've a point I wish proven and that wallet must stay closed or my argument is nil. I'll write soon and explain it all—just now I have to study some Government.

All grades are up and will be sent next time. Passed all exams—3.67 Nav—and have 3.0 or over in everything.

Much love for all

Frank

SUNDAY 31 MARCH 1935

Dear Mother and Dad and Joan

Well, the job of getting this Lucky Bag off to the printer is nearly finished. This morning we are getting off the rest of the athletics section and will follow that up with the Departments Section. This afternoon we will finish up the last of the Activities with the exception of one sig [signature] that we won't be able to get off till sometime next week. That's because that Sig contains the Musical Club's show and we won't be able to get the pictures for that until they get the costumes for it. Then, with everything off there won't be a thing left but the press's O.K.'s

They aren't difficult . . . just checking to see that everything is all right. I'm really a bit afraid to finish the thing and be deprived of a lot of my activity. It may have a bad effect. You see, I'm used to driving things along no matter what happens. With the book finished I won't have anything upon which I can expend all that energy and I'm afraid I'll be rather lost for awhile until I can get used to having a lot of time to do a few things and become accustomed to the inactivity. . . .

This must be all for this time. . . . Pretty busy this weekend, but it will soon be over with a sharp, quick, jerk . . . maybe next Thursday . . .

Much love for all,

Frank

POSTMARK 5/3/35

Dear Mother and Dad and Joan—

This may be the last letter from the Academy and due to pretty much of a rush hereabouts, it will have to be short.

First, Mother, no studs. I do appreciate your thoughts on getting them, or planning to—appreciate more than I can say, but I've already a set in uniform outfits (a regulation set) and besides, I want you to keep whatever they'd be for yourself. Remember, please, nothing for me, no graduation presents whatsoever—from anyone. Tell the girls about that and anyone who might feel this graduation called for some expression. I have everything I need and want for absolutely nothing but to have you three down here.

Dad, do you suppose Jim Wheeler or Arty Thompson would know where, or if, I could locate a little sailboat for the month I'll be home? It's just a thought, in lieu of a ballsey piece of automotive machinery.

I'm enclosing a telegram and some odds and ends—they mean more to you than they do to me—for the sake of possible future use tho', I'd like you to save the letters.

The two companies who offered me jobs have written since I turned them down saying "navy for a few years" and they both want me to get in touch with them as soon as I come out. It'll be a cinch to keep in touch with them in the meantime, so I guess (tho' not too strongly) that I have a job just waiting for me when I get out.

All for now—hurry down—

Much love for all—

Frank

POSTMARK 5/17/35

Dear Mother and Dad

If you have any regard for your wayward son's sanity please find out about Mac's Army trunk for me. If he can spare it for the space of about a month, please have it sent down, for I need something in which to send home my good uniforms. If it's available I wish you'd send it right down by express—you see I have some things I can pack right now and as they keep coming the need for space in a trunk will become more apparent.

The dope is now that Norm and I will be making a special trip to Washington in the Admiral's car to give the President and the Secretary of the Navy their copies of the book. I don't know how good it is tho' but it would be a good way to get away for a weekend.

We may get to go this coming weekend—and Hap's planning to come down the next, and the next is June Week, and the next is home—so things aren't shaping up so badly.

I want this to go right off now so will run along. And by the way, I've been asked to write articles for the Rochester Times Union and the Scholastic Editor—both concerning Lucky Bag—may turn into an efficiency expert (heaven forbid!)

Much love for all,
Frank

CHAPTER 12

What a Game!

The Letters of Gerald P. Motl

"What a grind. As soon as we got here people started hollering." Gerry Motl's impression of plebe summer jumps right off the page. "When the 2nd classmen want to haze you, no matter what you do is wrong. The best bet is to stay in your room. . . ."

An athlete with a seemingly endless supply of energy and enthusiasm, Motl's letters convey the fast-moving schedule of a USNA student: "I missed baseball for the last few days because of choir"; "the movie 'PT 109' is playing tonite"; and "Could you send me a box of regular sized bandaids and a roll of 1" adhesive tape. I need them to fix up my many injuries."

A varsity football player, Motl recorded football scores and details of games from the very beginning. "We beat Penn State today 21–8. . . . Last week I helped carry Roger Staubach around the mess hall." With absolute frankness, he told his parents, "I'm really messing up on the football team." The "messing up," always short-lived, did not deter him from playing. And in his senior year, he was instrumental in leading Navy to victory in the 1967 Army–Navy game.

A former nuclear submarine officer and a retired captain in the U.S. Naval Reserve, Gerry maintains close connections to the academy, returning to Annapolis whenever he can. He lives in Cincinnati with his wife, Roxanne, and two children, Christine and Brian. Today he is vice president for business development at Science Applications International Corporation.

2 JULY 1964

Dear Family,

What a grind. As soon as we got here people started hollering. We had to run everywhere, wait in line, etc. I got my uniform late. And now they have to be stencilled.

What a job.

When the 2nd classmen want to haze you, no matter what you do is wrong. The best bet is to stay in your room—leaving only when going to the john. It's worst when a bunch of them are together. Then they try to see who's the meanest. They yell as loud as they can and then I get flustered and they yell some more.

Before every function, we have to assemble and then march. I don't really go for it. It's so hot here—about 90. These white sailor outfits are baggy but thick. I've never sweat so much in my whole life. And then the forms to fill out! Yesterday I really felt like quitting. I thought the service wasn't for me. But everybody feels that way. When I go to bed at night, I feel like I've accomplished something. I hope I can stick it out. I've by no means got it made.

The square meals start Monday. The food is real good. Yesterday I had to sit next to the 2/c man. They have to be served everything first. I had to ask them if they wanted seconds and everything.

Our squad leader yells "plebe ho" and everyone in these rooms beats their " " into the corridor no matter what they're doing.

So far I've tried to keep myself as inconspicuous as possible. I'm doing alright. Some guys really get it. Word has it that as of yesterday 30 guys dropped out.

I'm getting used to the early hours. And I'm sleeping better. I'm going to start going to weekday mass because I need all the prayers I can get.

I was late for morning meal formation because I wrote this. I had to shave closer, shower again, and do pushups. I'm almost afraid to leave my room.

At breakfast I was next to the 2/c man again, but another guy is going to be there this afternoon.

We're supposed to clean our room but we haven't got a broom. There are coke machines downstairs but I haven't had an opportunity to get a glass yet. I'll try today.

July 4th and Sunday are holidays. I suppose we'll still be hazed.

Tell Tom W. that I'll write when I get the chance.

Gerald P. Motl *Courtesy* The Lucky Bag/*USNA Nimitz Special Collections*

I'll have to send my clothes home soon.

I'm getting a little homesick but there's not much time for it.

Say hello to everybody.

I miss you all. Write soon and pray for me cause I need it.

Gerry. MIDN USN

18 JULY 1964

Howdy,

Well, I made it through another week—and what a week. I just finished my extra duty this morning.

I had to (for the last 2 days) get up at 4:30 AM. Everyone else is sleeping, no noise, and pitch black out. "Ring" . . . goes the alarm clock, and then 5:15 we start running, calisthenics—and it is not easy (even for me). And if you don't work or loaf, you're put on a special squad that doesn't get any credit for even going out. So they have to come the next day. Well. At least that's over.

Yesterday, during drill, I was put on the "goon platoon". So I had to do some extra work with the rifles. I have a big blister on my toe and raw heels from the backs of my boondocks. My feet should heal by Monday, I hope.

I missed baseball for the last few days because of choir. I heard he cut all but 3 from the field I was on so I didn't bother to go back. I just signed up for rugby. It's like football, only without pads.

If I didn't tell you before, the choir is a really good deal. They make 3 trips a year, 2 to Washington and 1 to New York. And I'm in for sure. The plebes get liberty when they go. They've got a big ship out in the Bay, and all the plebes have to visit her. I'm going tomorrow because I have choir practice.

I'm getting in trouble for doing things I don't do. At infantry, the guy next to me made a mistake and I got two comearounds. I got another for having my eyes out of the boat when they weren't.

The movie "PT 109" is playing tonite. I plan on going if I can get this room cleaned up.

I've got to sleep with my rifle tonight because my squad leader kicked it out of my hands.

Could you send me a can or box of regular sized bandaids and a roll of 1" adhesive tape. I need them to fix up my many injuries.

I like to get mail every day (some kids get 4 or 5 letters) so write often and pray hard.

Gerry

14 AUGUST 1964

Hi:

Sorry I haven't written sooner but things have really been jumping. Our squad leader, an ex-marine, is really tough. Those comearounds we have every day are really bad. Everybody else gets them as punishment. Our squad has to go to them "to get used to it." He lets us out 4 minutes before formation soaking with sweat. But he is getting us "squared away."

Sunday we went to a picnic across the river. We played football and had lunch. I felt a little sick after twelve glasses of lemonade.

Yesterday we left the academy for the first time in 6 weeks 2 days. We saw the Orioles play in Baltimore. 16 busses took half the plebe class. I spent two bucks on food. The Orioles scored 5 runs before they even had the first out.

I drew my football gear a couple of days ago. I gave the guy my name and he went through a pile of cards . . . and one had my name on it (not everybody's). So I got pretty good equipment.

I got an inflamed tendon in my arm from rugby and a badly sprained thumb from boxing. The doctor told me to soak them four times a day for 30 minutes (slim chance!) I hope they'll be OK by Tuesday. There's a meeting for football Monday. I hope I make it.

We're starting to qualify in the knockabouts (sail boats). Parents weekend we can go out. At least 2 qualifieds have to be on the boat so I got a guy from Oregon whose parents aren't coming to sail with us. It's really a riot.

Mom, for comearounds, we run laps, do pushups, squat thrusts and everything. Believe me, it's harder than it sounds.

I think you should leave for here earlier so you have more time to get here safely. There's no need to rush.

If you want to bring me something parents weekend, make it an alarm clock, and a big bag of big, juicy oranges. YUM, YUM.

Those fizzies tablets are OK. If you've got them, send them. I'm still waiting for the Wyler's lemonade.

We knocked off the first place team in rugby 2 days ago and tied for the championship. We played off today (I couldn't play because of my injuries) and we lost 11–0. (We would have lost anyway)

Believe it or not, I haven't got fried the whole week. But you never know what the next day brings.

I talked to one of the ensign football coaches. I received some encouraging statements. If my injuries hold out, and with plenty of prayers and luck, I just might make it. Keep praying—

Sunday I'm going to sleep a lot so I am rested up for the first week.

Send me the money for my books when you sell them. I'll keep you posted.

Gerry

SUNDAY 6 SEPTEMBER 1964

Hi:

Well, Parent's Weekend is over. As soon as you left we started getting crapped on. We had a real hard comearound after supper—about a half hour. Had to go in the hallways with the mattresses, etc. It kind of woke us up to reality.

This week, we've been going to classes, mainly for introduction. My courses are 1) Engineering Drawing & Descriptive Geometry 2) Calculus & Analytic Geometry 3) English 4) Chemistry 5) Ocean Environment and Astronomy. A lot of math. Boy, have I got a pile of books.

I'm in a new room. My roommates are a little out of it. I'm the leader, kind of. I've got to tell them what to do.

We've got some nice guys in our company (from what I can tell now). They try to help us.

And guess what—of the hundreds of rooms in Bancroft Hall, Shue is 4 doors down!! I hope he spoons me. Our room is completely surrounded by upperclass.

Right now things are in a lull, easy—with the weekend, etc. I played football and went swimming today with Russ. Tomorrow we have liberty in the morning and afternoon. Then, the — hits the fan.

I'm trying to get squared away now—fix caps. Shoes, uniform, room—know reef points, etc. How successful I am I find out when the brigade gets back Tuesday.

I really enjoyed Parents Weekend. But now there are 104 days till Christmas leave.

I missed mass today because I was on watch. I'd like to go tomorrow but don't know if I will.

My new room overlooks the reflection pool. It's kind of neat.

I watched the football team in a practice scrimmage. Roger is pretty good. By the way, Army is picked to beat us. B.S.

Well, in case I don't get a chance to write before then ???, I'll see you at Christmas.

Pray hard,

Gerry.

1 NOVEMBER 1964

Hi:

Boy, did we lose to Notre Dame. But, let me tell you, they deserve to be #1 in the nation—quite a team. We had to get up at 4:30, eat breakfast and make sandwiches for lunch, and jump on the bus. There was milk and candy bars on the bus. We just bummed around before the game. You remember Tom Regner who played for St. Joe when I was a junior. Well, he tackled Roger a few times. They outweighed us 30 lbs a man in the line.

After the game Russ and I ate and started looking for some parties but after about 2 hours we ended up at the place we were first (after a pizza). It was a Notre Dame cocktail party. It really wasn't too cool because most of the girls were older and taken and there were a lot of adults. But then we met these 2 guys who we were talking to and finally a third guy— "Sarge". He was kind of a drunk—what a riot. He was telling us how he took Arthur Murray dancing lessons because he wants to be an expert. He and some other guys were buying beer ($.85 a crack) because mids rate. In the end of the evening things started livening up a bit, so it wasn't really too bad.

It's 11:00 a.m. and I'm in bed writing this. I have three big tests Monday and Tuesday—have to study—make a poster—finish library project and go to a tea fight this afternoon. I'm hurting.

In this week's batt game we won 22–0!! I caught 3 or 4 passes for about 70 or 80 yards, ran the ball here and there, made a few tackles and made the 2 pt conversion. I set up a few scores. We had carry on for a day—great.

Mom, the Trident calendars won't come out for another few weeks but I'll send you one when they do.

Dad, I won't take Spanish until next year.

Roger's trouble is his achilles tendon in his foot. He's got a special shoe. It just isn't real strong yet. His main trouble is a small line.

I'm looking forward to seeing Father—right now I have to get a little studying done and that poster. I'll run down to the steerage later and get some donuts seeing I don't have to go to lunch. Mass is at 5:30.

Keep praying,
Gerry

58 days

13 FEBRUARY 1965

Hi:

I made it through this week. It got off to kind of a bad start. But now things have more or less eased off. I don't know if you have ever heard of "100th night" but it's the 100th night before graduation. On that night, we get to have the firsties come around to us for about half an hour—big deal. But they have a "buildup" which means we get run till then. Some is fun but some is a pain in the ass. I asked a real fruit guy around so I'll be alright. But some guys have to bring around all their shelves at morning and night. Well, at least when it's over, plebe year is supposed to get easier. It's March 1st.

I got a valentine from Mary and Jeanne but got no chance to get them anything. Buy them a box of candy or something and say it's from me, OK?

By the way I saw Shoen today. He's leaving Monday cause he flunked out. Reishl and Frymark are unsat and Russ didn't make Sup's list cause he got a D in Phys Ed.

Tell Lex that if he goes Air Force, he's crazy.

I'm studying tonight so I can go into town for a little while tomorrow since I rate liberty.

Frymark and I went into town to confirm the car deal. We should have a real good time. We get off Saturday at noon and have to be back Monday night. We're going to DC. Don't worry. We'll be careful.

My overload had better get more interesting or I'll drop it.

Right now I'm listening to a tape of "South Pacific" in the library. Really great.

Dad, thanks for the LIFE.

You know, I've noticed that I'm hardly ever relaxed now unless I have study behind me. It's like I'm under pressure to keep it up. I tried to tell myself I was just going to enjoy myself this weekend—but what am I doing now?—studying.

I can't wait till we get carry on. Then I can study during the week and have fun on weekends.

By the way again, last week, the big scorer on the fieldball team was at West Point. So guess who was tied for leading scorer with 3 goals—me.

Keep writing and praying.

Maybe I'll call you from DC Saturday. Pray hard.

Gerry

5 JUNE 1965

Hi:

June Week has begun. Yesterday afternoon it started with the big dress parade. After the parade, I took this Cdr.'s daughter to that choir picnic. With bermudas. Boy did it feel funny wearing civies in the hall. The picnic was neat. It was across the river where we had a picnic last summer. They had soda, hamburgers, hot-dogs, ice-cream, potato chips, apples, bananas. Some guys were singing and playing guitars. We left there and went to the field house to hear Serendipity singers. (They play on Hootenanny sometimes). Then my roommate and I and the girls went to this informal hop in Dahlgren Hall. The "Spiffies" (midshipmen) were playing. They're great (better than most regular bands). We went to get something to eat and then ended up guess where?? At McDonald's. We got back about 12:30. What an exhausting day.

This morning I just slept for a while. My roommate and girls and I went out to eat and then went to the lacrosse game. We squashed Army 18–7. We also beat them in track.

I have to go on stupid watch tonite and the next day (I'm getting $15). Second Class ring dance is tonite.

Next Thursday at about 5 AM, I'll leave for San Diego.

I got Math A, Chem A, Phy A, Bull A[,] Command C = 3.67. You should be getting my ranking and stuff before long.

The weather here is real nice. June Week is great. There's always something to do. As a matter of fact, there's too much to do.

I'll write again before I go on cruise.

Gerry

9 SEPTEMBER 1965

Hi:

Well, back for number 2. I had to go to watch squad inspection when I got back. I didn't get fried though ten guys did.

Basically all we've been doing is getting things squared away—rigging up uniforms, books and getting the room squared away.

I'm going to try to see Daley and Van Sant tonite. I hear that a guy from Waukesha is in my company.

You remember those privileges that I was telling you about. Well 2, cars and late nights, were rebuked. Boy does that make me mad.

My subjects are:

Calculus with Elements of Statistical Interference
Matrix Theory
Physics
Modern European History
Spanish
Modern American Lit (about a dozen novels & plays)

I'll really have to kill myself to get stars.

I'm not giving the plebes any static. I'm pretty nice to them.

It's really funny down at the tables watching all the crap they take. It's really funny.

Well, there's not much more to say.

Do you still want tickets for the Notre Dame game?

By the way, thanks a lot for being so nice this summer. I know I didn't do anything constructive and was probably a big burden. Mom, thanks for the bacon, lettuce and tomatoes and Dad, thanks for the lettuce ($) and the understanding concerning my episodes in Hoyt.

Well write often
(I still like mail)
Gerry

2 OCTOBER 1965

Hi:

Again—another week is over. I didn't do red hot or real bad on any tests. You know I haven't got an A since classes started. The highest I can manage is a B. Report cards will be out in a couple weeks. I'll probably have over a 3 but almost sure below 3.4.

We had our batt football game Thursday. After missing two practices because of watch. I thought I was in disfavor. Well, I started at left cornerbacker. Well, needless to say, I was the day's leading receiver and I was playing defense. What I'm trying to say is, at the cost of being boastful, I intercepted two passes. It was a defensive game. We won 6–0 on a score in the last quarter. Right now I lead the Brigade in interceptions (after 1 game??)

And dad, what's the story cutting down our football team. For a team that isn't ranked, we're doing damn well. Syracuse is rated the best in the East and Stanford was in the top 15 before we tied them. I'm going to see the game today over closed circuit TV.

Our "privileges" are undergoing the effects of a reactionary period. Not only were all our new privileges wiped out, but now we're going backwards. As it was, I was off from Friday afternoon to Sunday nite if I took a weekend Army game. Now, weekends start after the end of the game. A day of liberty wasted for no reason. They got us in a vice and they keep closing it. I wish Kaufman would leave. He's living in the old world.

I won't be going to Notre Dame—too much $ and 24 hours on a bus. I can't see that.

Well, Sat noon formation is upcoming so I've got to get ready.

Dad, I just sent you some magazines and other stuff at the store.

Well, see ya.

Gerry

11 FEBRUARY 1966 FRIDAY NITE

Hi:

I'm writing this from the Brigade library. It's 10 after 10 right now. Right now I'm experiencing a typical bunch of Navy good deals

1. There's a purge on in the company for keeping rooms perfect. A bunch of guys got fried today.

2. The whole company is getting inspected tomorrow by our company officer.

3. This, the whole brigade is steaming about. You know, Army weekend the Lettermen are going to be here. Originally, it was going to be civilian attire (a sweater hop) with a Spiffy hop afterward. Not anymore. The uniform now is regular shoes, drill trou, reg shirt, black tie & reg navy (ugly) sweater. And now a stinking Chief's Band is playing for the dance. What a farce. All because some big wheel is coming down that weekend. Some day the world's going to find out what a front this place puts up. Boy, am I mad.

I've got a new roommate. Paul Willoughby the same guy I roomed with last year—a real nice guy. Especially after the two bombs I had before. One of my old roommates snored like you Dad (only worse!!)

Academics this semester are the hardest yet. I'm studying during the day + 5 hours at night.

Anything new about coming out for spring leave? Two youngsters from Wisconsin are out. One guy (went to Wis Rapids Assumption—4.0 QPR) quit and another guy got the boot. A bunch of my friends have left.

The snow is really melting quick. I'm still planning on going out for football. (If my thumb isn't broken—I was playing catch with some guys on the team the other day. I think it might be.)

Well, not much else to say. I'm hanging on till June '68. (Our rings are on display).

Gerry

25 FEBRUARY 1966

Hi:

As I write this letter I am in a state of confusion. I still don't know about football. It should start next Tuesday. But my thumb is still a dilemma. I've got to get another X-ray Saturday (tomorrow) to see what the story is. I saw my other x ray. My thumb is broken in two places—one is old, from high school days. If I do play, it'll have to be taped. The cards were stacked against me from the beginning for not playing for two years—but now it'll be even worse. All I can do is try.

As I may have mentioned before, my marks aren't going to be red hot this time. I'm sure I can bring them up though if I buckle down. The grades should be out sometime next week.

As far as Spring Leave is concerned, it starts earlier than it says in the calendar—12:00 Wed, 23 March. So I suppose that will affect your plans. We can hang around Annapolis for the rest of the day if you want—eat at the Harbor House and make plans from there. As you know, leave ends at 5:30 Sunday nite. (Maybe you'd like to eat in the messhall that nite, Dad). Sorry, Mom, no girls allowed.

This weekend is Army weekend. We're (the Cath Choir) going to sing Sunday with the Rosemont College Choir. We're supposed to drag them this weekend—with the Lettermen, this, and other complications too numerous to mention, the weekend promises to be quite a mix-up.

The choirs have been tape-recorded and filmed. I guess we're going to be on national television to portray a different image of the Academy.

Not much more to say—I'll probably call Sunday—before you get this.

Looking forward to seeing you,
Gerry

1 SEPTEMBER 1966

Hi:

Well, here it is the big report. We practiced Monday and Tuesday. Monday 3 guys ahead of me got hurt—so I've been playing 2nd team for the last 2 days.

Monday we got filmed on pass defense. I got zapped 3 times for not reading my keys, but I lead in interceptions.

We had a scrimmage yesterday. The first big one of the year. It was closed to the press and the public.

I was with the second unit. I did pretty good—read my keys better and I tackled a guy for safety on the second play from scrimmage and then made an interception when they got to our ten yard line.

Today I was back to 3rd team cause the sick guys came back. But now they'll keep 9 backs. One out of my string and I'm in hot contention. I think I have the nod but Saturday we have a huge scrimmage in the stadium. That will determine whether I get V or JV.

The food is great—all to make you strong—no desserts.

I'm going to Dick Evert's house again—from Saturday noon to Monday noon.

The brigade has to be back Wed.

Russ stopped in and said hello.

Well—pray for Saturday. That's the day.

Gerry

4 SEPTEMBER 1966

Hi:

This is just a progress report. Well, there was a cut and I made it. There are now 10 defensive backs and I'm one of them. There are 5 corner-men and 5 safeties. Maybe that's it? I know they'll only take 8 to away games.

Coach Elias has been "shitting" on me for the last two days. Yesterday, he said, "Motl, you're a nip-shit." Dad, they know I'm here.

The kick-off team was up today. I'm the first sub at 8 of the 11 positions. That's a good sign. So???

Practice is hard and so are my courses. Something will probably give. But I'll do my best.

Pray please,
Gerry

18 SEPTEMBER 1966

Hi,

Needless to say, WE WON 27–7. What an outstanding game. On the opening kick off I was in. I was the first guy to hit him, then he broke the tackle, kind of and then someone really struck him and he fumbled and we recovered. Then we got penalized on the one—well you can read about it.

I made another tackle on the kick off. Then in the fourth quarter I went in on regular defense. Corso told me only to call rotates, taking no account for field position. I think he thought I was going to clutch. Any way I was kind of nervous when I got in but I didn't do anything wrong. But then we were rotated my way and I was right on the flanker. I wasn't supposed to let him go inside but he did. Anyway, I had to stick with him then. He caught and bobbled the ball while the LB and me were coming towards him at 50 mph from different directions. Well he (the BC bum) moved or something just as I was reaching for him, our LB smashed right into me. He got another ten yards before I tackled him luckily. Anyway the LB gashed his eye and I couldn't breathe—got hit right in the solar plexus. So with my big chance, I had to come out of the game. There was only 2 mins left so they didn't put me back in. What a game!

I just get a B robe and a parka for the Army and the Air Force games. Do you want to come out to the Army game? Tom Daley played too.

I'm dragging this weekend a girl who I met at Dick Evert's house. I'm going to call you at noon so I guess I should close.

I probably won't be going to Dallas next week. They take exactly 2 teams I guess.

My grades may drop but you know how it is.

Pray Navy goes 11–0 (Bowl included)

Gerry

19 SEPTEMBER 1964 11:40 PM 2340

Hi:

We beat Penn State today 21–8! Now we get to carry on till Sunday night. Last week I helped carry Roger Staubach around the mess hall.

I was first in the library for about four hours catching up. I'm falling behind, so I've really got to start working.

Thursday, we had a good pep rally—neat.

There's not really much to write—it's just the same old grind.

Send me the clippings from all the Marquette football games.

I hope all is working well in our new enterprise. Dad, give me your address when you go up north so I can write.

Oh yeah, I'm out for Batt football. I'm pretty good compared to a lot of guys. If I keep working I'll probably go both ways.

I asked Tom to come to the Army game seeing he's going to come up for Thanksgiving the same weekend. I was on watch today which pretty well ruined it. All my liberty? Was shot.

Tom Liesner, from Whitefish Bay High, scored the last TD for us today. Next week is homecoming. It should be pretty good. Well, keep praying and so will I.

See you in 91 days.

Gerry

24 SEPTEMBER 1966

Hi

I'm listening to the Navy–SMU game right now. We're losing 14–3. It doesn't look good.

Cartwright, our first team QB, got hurt in the first quarter and we've been using the 2nd stringer since. SMU has a great team.

The reason I'm not travelling is because they only take the first 2 teams exactly. And that's not me. I guess I have to wait till someone gets hurt before I travel.

On the kick off last week, I got credit for making the first tackle all alone causing the fumble too. Imagine I was the leading tackler for Navy. That didn't last long. In addition, I got credit for two assists in 2 of the other 4 kick-offs. Well, I still didn't travel. Many people were surprised—now I can catch up on my studies.

The way it stands now I go along with the varsity in everything. I get a scouting report and have to know it, but I don't travel until something happens.

SMU just scored again. Score now 21–3. It's hopeless now. I guess. SMU just intercepted on our 1st play. It's hopeless. When Cartwright got hurt, that was it. We just intercepted back again.

I've got to write to Jim Wheeler. He wrote me a letter and asked me to get him 4 tickets to Army. I get 4 free tickets to every game since I'm on the varsity—so I can get you 4 of the best seats in the house. But please tell me for sure if you're coming to Army or not. No backing out.

Pray we start playing good.

Gerry

P.S. Daley and Van Sant both traveled because 2 guys got hurt.

14 OCTOBER 1966 FRIDAY NITE 11:45

Hi

As you may know I didn't make the trip again. We play Pitt tomorrow. I think we'll win for a change. From what I understand not the whole varsity will suit up for our home games. All didn't last time either. So, I guess it's not sure whether I'll be playing—although I can't see one reason why I shouldn't be. I was one of the best extras out there, I think. Well, I'll most likely play so there's no sense moaning about it.

By the way, I've got a subscription to the Log for you—now you'll get every one and I won't have to mail them.

I'm going down to Mary Washington College with Dick Evert tomorrow. He knows a girl down there. His father will pick us up after formation, then we'll take him home—and then take off. It'll be good to get away from here.

I may not be the best football player on the team but I've got the best grades by a long shot. Some guys are really hurting—but that's understandable if you travel every weekend.

Don't forget to get those reservations—until I'm sure. I'll probably call Sunday to say Hello.

I'm signed up for the Chicago Charter again. And I ordered 6 tickets to Army for Jim Wheeler. Your seats will probably be next to his so you can say hello.

Keep praying,

Gerry

21 OCTOBER 1966 FRIDAY NITE

Hi,

It's Friday nite right now. Tomorrow we play William and Mary. I'm playing. They're only suiting up 9 defensive backs this week—I'm right under the wire—and I'm on the kick off team again. Yesterday I sprained my ankle slightly. It shouldn't bother me at all when it's taped.

Most mids think this is going to be an easy game tomorrow—but it won't. W & M has their best team in years—and they've got a great QB. We'll win big if everyone puts out. Otherwise? That N.D. game should be a great one—but we're not worrying about that now.

Homecoming is this weekend.—lots of grads around. We've got to do good tomorrow.

I saw Russ the other day—I don't know if I told you that. Are you travelling in the same car with the Linstedts? Are you staying in the same place? Any chance of Waldow making the trip with you?

Nothing much else has been happening. I'll call you Sunday—so you'll hear from me before you get this letter.

Pray we did good Saturday (me, too)

KILL 'EM

Gerry

10 NOVEMBER 1966

Hi,

Tomorrow is a holiday so I thought I'd write to you tonite instead of this weekend. I have some good things to say and some bad.

First, I did real good on mid terms and I think I'll have about a 3.70.

But, I'm really messing up on the football team. Monday, everybody who wasn't a starter had a big scrimmage with the poolies. I made lots of little mistakes and generally did only a fair job (although I did make a good interception). Anyway, on Tuesday I just stepped in for a few goal line plays and I didn't pinch tight enough and a guy got by me. So Elias goes into a damn big production, "Well, Motl, that was a cardinal sin," etc. Anyway, his criticism was anything but constructive. Well, that really got me—screwed up my poise and everything. Well, as a result I've been messing up all week so it looks like I'll see you in Philly Friday nite. I'm generally down and pretty frustrated. You know, "What the hell."

Actually, as far as I'm concerned, just between you and me, Elias may not be long for Navy. Two lousy years in a row don't go. Well, all I can hope is a fair chance for next year.

Russ said he can't get out of taking care of the plebes. He is crazy. I don't know what he lives for.

I wrote to Waldo today. I'll call before the Army game to get all the details in. I hope you know Waldo and I will be staying with you Friday night. We can sleep on the floor or something.

Well, pray for me

Gerry

CHAPTER 13

To Truly Witness for Christ

The Letters of Barry Mason Shambach

"As you have probably noticed, this experience had quite a profound effect on me. I received the booklet 'Ten Steps to Christian Maturity' . . . and am finding the reading/study very interesting, stimulating and challenging." Within a few months of having written these words, Barry Mason Shambach would submit his resignation from the academy. Today, the Reverend Mason Shambach serves the Westlake Presbyterian Church in Battle Creek, where he has been pastor since 1982.

Entering the U.S. Naval Academy in 1967 from Shelbyville, Indiana, Shambach wrote a weekly newsletter to his family and friends. Sometimes, he'd add personal handwritten notes. The letters in this collection are ones that Shambach sent to his friend back home, John Kemper.

The letters supply details about Glee Club and Protestant Choir, as well as the tense atmosphere following the assassination of the Reverend Martin Luther King Jr. Today, rereading these letters, Shambach says, "I do wish my letters better reflected the current events of the day—but we were rather immersed in Academy life." That very immersion makes the letters interesting.

Since leaving the academy, the Reverend Shambach continues to serve the navy as a reserve duty chaplain and as a blue and gold officer. He is married with two children.

SUNDAY 20 AUGUST 1967

Dear John,

If you can't read this I'll just have to pound a little harder or buy new carbon, and since new carbon costs money—

The past week has gone pretty fast for a change, but the weekend is going even faster. The sun was shining brightly all week for every period of infantry (which is getting to be a real pain). So now during my very limited free time, it's pouring down rain. I guess the Navy has finally taken care of the weather here along with everything else.

We only had two classes in Naval Science this week—both in racing the Academy's 24' Knockabout sailboats. Monday we have a company elimination race: the winner will compete against boats from 11 other companies Tuesday. In practice racing[,] my boat (crew of 5) didn't do too well, but we had a lot of fun in near collisions with other boats. The second day we were so far behind the other boats coming in to the harbor that we had to get a tow from a motor launch (which, incidentally, makes docking much easier). Our main problem is lack of coordination among the members of the crew—5 is too many for Knockabout racing anyway. But, who knows—we may do all right with a few breaks.

In a P.T. (Physical Training) class this week we played rugby—an unforgettable experience with a wildly rugged sport. Rugby is sort of like "Kill the Man with the Ball" (I use the word kill loosely, but for emphasis); no player can block or even touch any man that doesn't have the ball, but he can smash the ballcarrier, who has to lead his team down the field at all times. The game never stops unless the ball goes out of bounds, so it's a game of terrific endurance (or lack of it).

In the weekly P-rade our company finished a disappointing 6th—so no slack in infantry this next week. However, looking at the bright side of things, our battalion basketball team won its first (and last) game this week; our season record (back to gloominess) was an unbelievable 1–9. All I can say about the season is "No excuse, Sir." for we had the material. Again however, I was selected for the all star B-ball team along with 2 other players from our team; I think the all star game is to be played Parents' Weekend.

At Wed. noon meal formation the contestants for the Miss World title watched us march from the main steps of Bancroft Hall. The big disappointment was that we didn't get the opportunity to watch them; they weren't even introduced to the 4th Class Regiment. I guess our higher ups must have figured that complete pandemonium would have broken

Barry Mason Shambach *Courtesy the Reverend Mason Shambach*

forth if we poor, deprived plebes had been allowed to gaze upon such feminine beauty after 7 weeks of excommunication from girls. At any rate we felt the whole set up was entirely unfair (they could see us, but we couldn't see them) and very discriminatory (but, oddly enough, we haven't had any protest marches)

I was on watch Wed. evening so missed the wrestling semi-finals. Our Batt (2nd) is pretty short on wrestlers, I guess, since we didn't get anybody into the finals. . . .

The Starboard Battalion (1st, 2nd and 3rd battalions) Talent Show was held Thurs night in Mahan Hall. Some of the numbers were really good and the entertainment was a welcome relaxation from our hectic schedule. On the other hand, some of the acts could have used more practice and variety; thus I was unfairly disappointed with some of the performances, especially since I felt I didn't have the time to work up an act and didn't even try out. Along the lines of entertainment, I really appreciate the SHS Show Group more and more after being a part of the audience for various types of entertaining groups. Show Group, and the opportunity to entertain on stage, is something (along with girls) that I feel the lack of here so far and look back on with fond memories. (Even though it really hasn't been any length of time that I've been separated from either).

On the basis of a reading test, I was put into the Academy Protestant Chapel Choir, which means I have a chance to try out for Glee Club (being in Chapel Choir is a prerequisite). There is also an Antiphonal Choir that rehearses separately and performs independently of the Chapel Choir. The two do joint numbers sometimes, but traditionally like to remain separate. I'm told there is quite a bit of rivalry between the two.

On Sat (yesterday) afternoon my brother and father arrived here for the last 45 minutes of visiting hours. They brought the new Gibson guitar that was purchased for me with graduation gift money and my own resources. It's a fine instrument and has a truly beautiful tone. I made a deal with my roommate that he can play it anytime as long as he gives me some instruction on how to play. We sing together in our free time and in between classes (while we change clothes—er—uniforms) for some real relaxation and tension-easing. Since he isn't a movie fiend, either, it's pretty nice that he both sings and plays the guitar (also since we don't rate TV's, radios, record players, or tape recorders)

Since I ran on to another page, I suppose I may as well try to fill it up (with millions of mistakes as in previous pages).

On personal grooming—we have to get a haircut (regulation burr, that is) once a week and can be fried for not doing so. We also have to shave every morning with the same "not so hairy" consequence of demerits for failure to do so. We average 4 or 5 showers a day (and 6–7 clothes changes) so BO isn't much of a problem. In fact, they (Our higher-up's dermatologist) tell us that deodorant doesn't do that much good if you wash twice a day and since we're presently guinea pigs for an Academy soap test, we're instructed not to use deodorant—it could affect the results of the test. For any rash or ailment you can come up with, the Medical Department has a concoction or will brew one up and dole it out free of charge. We've had a full mouth X-ray and one check-up at Dental Quarters. Also, every 4th Classmen had a casting of his teeth made and from that "custom made" mouthguards; every participant in varsity or intramural sports such as football, lacrosse, soccer, basketball, etc. must wear his mouthguard. The mouthguard is the most comfortable I've ever worn and is hardly noticeable.

The facilities here at the Academy are very extensive and almost all are available to us. The only trouble is that we just don't have the time or endurance to take advantage of them all. In Macdonough Hall alone are squash and handball courts, wrestling mats, boxing rings and bags, a huge (indoor) swimming pool called the Natatorium—with 2 low boards, a high board (15' deep water). A gymnastics floor with all types of equipment, an instruction swimming pool, and a fencing loft. In the fieldhouse are an indoor track, squash courts, weight room. Two full length or 4 short basketball courts. Outside are numerous tennis courts, several large athletic fields and, of course, the boat dock of dinghies, knockabouts and yawls. In Bancroft Hall there are bowling alleys (we pay only for shoe rental), squash courts, and pool and ping pong tables (which we DON'T rate yet). So there is quite a bit to do on recreational liberty time (oh—also a golf course across the river—bus transportation), but, as I said, there just isn't enough time to use more than a few of the facilities. I'm planning to go bowling for the first time tonight. Also, for us all activities are NON-coeducational, and may I stress that the only times we have recreational liberty and can use all this stuff (other than in intramurals) is on Sat and Sun afternoons—when we have to recuperate from the last week and try to get some rest for the one to come (and type newsletters).

Well, since I polished shoes all yesterday afternoon waiting for my dad and brother and I haven't gotten any exercise today yet, I think I'll shove off to the squash courts for awhile. Also the bottom of this sheet is getting dangerously close. BYE !!!

John—since my parents aren't home this weekend and yours have been such faithful correspondents, I decided to send you this copy instead of some beautiful babe. Actually, you're about the only one who's written to me from S-ville with any regularity besides Bubbles Ewing—most of my writing correspondents are from other cities (that I met at church camp) and of course, Barbara Palacios. I'm going broke calling Barbara in Elizabeth New Jersey but I have to keep sane somehow. If we're still passing compliments, my roommate didn't want to read your letter either. Oh well, be good and don't loaf too much.

BMS

3 SEPT 67

Hi!!

It's the end of another l-o-n-g hard week (yeah!!) Last weekend was Parent's Weekend. I had a very enjoyable time showing my family around the Academy and letting them in on a little of academy life (the more pleasant aspects of it, that is) However, since I didn't get my usual weekend rest, this week has seemed a little harder than the previous ones.

The addition of football practice last Mon. contributed to mass fatigue. We did a lot of hitting all week to give the coaches an idea of who can play football and those that should be cut. Of the 320 that showed up in pads on Mon. about 120 are still practicing. I got a locker and blue jersey on Thurs. and started off with the second team at defensive right and on Sat. the first day they attempted to group us into teams. Not all of the guys are out in the locker room yet—only the first 4 strings: those who don't have a locker dress in their rooms and stow gear there, also. In the locker room we get pretty good service—clean T shirt, supporter, socks, and towel every day plus a coke after practice. On the other hand, my high school equipment was better than what I was issued here. Actually, practice hasn't been as exhausting as in high school. We hit harder and move more quickly, but we only go an hour and ½ as opposed to 2 hr. average at SHS. Of course I've played nothing but defense since we started, so my training at one position is more intensive. The fundamentals and techniques I'm practicing are all ones I've worked on before—a little rusty right now, but still very familiar. One last thing about practice—we don't have to work on conditioning as much as many teams as we're all in fairly good physical condition.

The evening lecture series this week has been a history of the US naval battles of the American revolution, Civil War, 1st and 2nd World Wars, plus our involvement in Vietnam today. The combined slide-lecture-movie presentation was for the most part very interesting, but staying awake for 2 straight hours seemed often more of a battle than that on the screen.

While I'm talking about staying awake—anytime someone gets drowsy in a class or lecture here, it's his responsibility to stand up and go to the back of the room to remain standing until he recovers sufficiently. This is a standard practice; lecturers and professors are easily upset by a midshipman's falling asleep and missing valuable material. I might also add that drowsiness is very common here with the schedule of much exercise and little sleep; thus this matter of sleeping through a class is discussed over and over and is punishable with demerits.

On Tues. afternoon we went across the river to see the Marines put on a vertical envelopment demonstration. It was very realistic and exciting (in addition to being expositive); the demonstration was of the operations involved in wiping out a Vietcong bunker. First a helicopter dropped a 4 man reconnaissance team down a rope as it hovered 100 ft above the ground. The recon team located the bunker (a sandbag barricade on the rifle range) and marked landing strips for 2 helicopters to land and drop off a 22 man assault team. Long range gun fire was simulated with blasts from buried charges as was the bombing of Huey helicopter as it made passes over the bunker. From the time the Marine assault team landed, they fired blanks from their weapons; rifles, machine guns, small rocket launcher, grenade launcher. When the enemy was almost beaten, a Marine closed in with a 50 yd flame thrower. The final attack on the bunker was made with bayonets fixed. I think the whole demo was worth the hr. wait.

We've been getting an introduction to engineering this past week, having a class in a different department each day. We also started a review slide rule and trig course on Thurs; the training with the slide rule is especially helpful.

On Fri each room was issued a $140 tape recorder for language tapes and also each midshipman received 5 tapes for his specific course. Since I need quite a bit of work on speaking and understanding speech in Spanish, this ought to be especially helpful. However, the tape recorders are to be used only for listening to the language tapes—an order not wisely broken. (Since we don't rate having our own recorders)

Yesterday we marched in a big Parade for the USNA Commandant Change of Command ceremony. Captain Hayworth relieved recently promoted Rear Admiral Kinney of his duty of commanding the Brigade of Midshipmen.

Early in the week (the exact night doesn't matter) we had more fun and games with our squad leaders. On this certain night we had a little free time, so our 2nd class leaders called us out for a Plebe Ho during which we had to stack all the shelves and clothes hangers from our lockers (on which all our clothes and gear were formerly stowed) in piles in the hall. After we stripped our pads and shoved them out into the hall, we were given 30 minutes to prepare for a formal inspection. To say the least, there was quite a bit of hurrying and scurrying around, but we made it in time (Whew!!)

Tomorrow we supposedly get the day off except for morning football practice and our chore of moving into academic year rooms in the evening.

Since the brigade reforms on Thurs. everybody's going to be busy brushing up on professional knowledge, preparing for the barrage of questions. I've 4 days to roast at the meal table before I get to go on training table (where we can eat like normal people) a week from Monday.

Tuesday my aunt, uncle, 3 daughters and enlisted Army friend come here for a relaxing picnic lunch and enjoyable Knockabout sailing. We had town liberty this afternoon and evening during which many guys have gone to a movie or done some shopping in town. I haven't taken advantage of the opportunity except to go to a very nice ice cream parlor with my aunt and uncle.

Several guys in my platoon have been having birthdays lately, so I've been especially good to my stomach with pieces of their cakes sent from home. It's a little strange that everybody who has goodies goes over to other guys' rooms to eat what they have—the cycle results in quite a variety of good eating for everyone.

The varsity football team has been practicing twice daily for 2 weeks now; it's the job of the 4th class to see that there's plenty of spirit and enthusiasm around them at all times. Thus anyone who isn't involved in a plebe fall sport right now (intramurals haven't started yet) is expected to be down in the practice field bleachers watching the varsity knock heads. It seems a little strange to me for 500 guys (plebes) to be cheering at a regular varsity football practice, but it's the Navy way. Also, the cheering in the mess hall has picked up since the football players came back early to start practicing.

Well, I want to get some rest before our (plebe) practice tomorrow morning (Labor Day). The amazing thing about this place is—EVERYBODY ON THE OUTSIDE'S TRYING TO GET IN, AND EVERYBODY ON THE INSIDE IS TRYING TO GET OUT!!!!!

Goodnight

John—Thanks again for the popcorn—it was really good. I imagine SHS just isn't the same without Mr. McKinley & Mr. Ingram!

Barry

SUN 10 SEPT 67

Hello!

Plebe Summer is over and the academic year has begun—which means 3000 upperclassmen are here to give us all the static they can, use us for personal servants—which they TECHNICALLY don't rate—and run us into the ground.

The first three days of last week finished up a brief slide rule and review trigonometry course. It was interesting and very helpful.

Starting Wed. we have been playing "puppet" for the upper classes. Tues. night we moved into our 3 man academic year room—I never realized we had so much gear until we had to move it all. My new roommate (in addition to Russ Shaw) is also from California; he's an aviation enthusiast who hopes to become an astronaut someday. (He was in a parachuting club and Civil Air Defense Patrol in high school).

Getting back to Wed—we plebes spent quite a bit of time on Wed. and Thurs cleaning up rooms for upperclassmen, including dusting, washing unbelievable crusty blinds, scrubbing bowls, washing windows and mirrors and scrubbing decks. I was surprised (pleasantly) at the appreciation the upperclass showed for our "voluntary" efforts, which really weren't too strenuous.

Thurs. evening we 4th Class ate our first meal with the Brigade—an experience which will long be remembered. At the standard table, 2 Firsties (college seniors) sit at one end, 2 2nd classmen (juniors) at the other end, 4 youngsters (sophomores) along one side; 4 Plebes get the HOT SEATS along the other side.

SAT. 16 SEP

Well, here goes another attempt to get this letter off—this one was interrupted Sun. afternoon by Fourth Class Chapel Choir practice. We Plebes are working on the Messiah at special practices Sun. afternoon. The Chapel Choir has sung it for the last few years, so the upperclass already know it.

To finish off about company meal tables—the food is always passed first to the Firsties, then to the 2nd class, to the youngsters, and finally to the plebes. This means that trays and bowls have to make 3 trips up and down the table to serve everybody. What few scraps are left for the plebes usually grow cold on their plates, for the plebes are either holding up serving dishes for seconds for the upper class or answering professional questions. More than a few of my classmates have lost 15 pounds since the beginning of academic year.

However, I'm on a training table for plebe football which is a real relief! There are no upper class at our table; we get to eat like normal people, and we get as much as we want to eat. (Our menu is often different from the regular company tables, which is usually good but sometimes—such as when pie is being served everybody else—is a little disappointing) When I asked one plebe football player why he was taking a box of dry cereal out of the mess hall, he said it was for his roommate who is on company tables starving to death.

This past week has been the most hectic so far—every spare minute I've had to spend studying, and I'm still behind in my work. Being on watch all day Monday, when I had 5 free periods to study really hurt me, and I didn't get caught up the rest of the week. Calculus is giving me the most trouble, but I hope to get straightened out a little before my next class. Besides our 17 hr. academic load, we have 2 periods of PT (physical training) and 2 periods of drill each week. My courses for the semester are: calculus (4 hrs), chemistry (4 hrs) Spanish (3 hrs), English composition (3 hrs) air, ocean and environment (essentially oceanography) 3 hrs, and PT and drill.

We have study hour every evening from 7:45 p.m. to 10:00 p.m. during which we have to be in our rooms and no upperclass are supposed to disturb us. Lights out is at 10:30 P.M. and we don't rate getting up until 5:30 a.m. (However, we sometimes have to get up a little earlier to study and get squared away for the day) We have morning comearounds 10 minutes every morning and ½ hr. plebe morning workouts every other morning for those who are guilty of petty errors.

The biggest event of this week for me was being selected for the Glee Club. Only 25 plebes are chosen for the 100 voice, all classes chorus that has appeared on TV shows such as the Ed Sullivan Show in recent years.

I'm still second string defensive right end on the plebe football team and still trying to move up. We had a filmed scrimmage on Sat. in which my team did a great job of giving up zero first downs, but in which I wasn't particularly outstanding—in fact, only 3 or 4 plays came my way.

Singing in the Chapel Choir is really inspiring and a lot of fun. The last two anthems we've sung we plebes read through only twice before singing them on Sunday before a congregation. The terrific thing about the choir is that everybody reads well and we learn music quickly.

After study hour almost every night we have "shower parties" at which the plebes gang up on an upperclassman who has had a birthday, has been engaged, or has been pinned in a wrestling match and throw him in the shower. Some of them are really lively and put up quite a struggle (but the 40 plebes of the mighty 10th Company always overcome)

Today (which is now Sunday) we spent all afternoon making a required poster for the Penn State game this Saturday. At the time it didn't seem quite as important as some of the other millions of things we have to do but as it turned out, we took second place in our company contest. So get carry on (no chopping in Bancroft Hall or bracing up at meals) until tomorrow noon and we get our poster put up in the Rotunda. By the way, by "we" I mean my two roommates and me.

Well time, tide and formation wait for no man—I do like it here a little more than during Plebe Summer—it seems more like an Academy than a boot camp. And as the upperclass tell us, the Naval Academy is a great place to be FROM!!!

John—I'm sending my parents' letter air mail at their request from now on, so you don't have to worry anymore. I thought my mother's description of watching everybody else get my carbons almost hilarious (but I guess they didn't) Well John, study hard and don't molest the girls.

Barry

P.S. If you can't read this don't worry—get a magnifying glass.

P.P.S. I'll get some new carbon paper soon.

SUN 24 SEPT 67

Well, it's Sunday night and another academic week is ready to take the place of an enjoyable weekend. NAVY had a great victory over Penn State 23–22 on Sat. afternoon here at the Academy. Navy went 70 yds. in the last minute and ½ of the game for the winning touchdown. I don't think Quarterback Cartwright threw an incomplete pass on the final TD drive. Our defense was a little weak in the first ½ but over all it looks like Navy is going to have a pretty exciting season.

Sat night Chad and Jeremy gave a 2 hr. concert. I went but left at the intermission, a little disappointed and very sleepy. Their music was okay, but it just didn't do too much for me. I didn't like their staging at all.

A P.S. on the football game—it was especially nice for us plebes, since we get carry on the rest of the weekend after the Navy victory.

On Wed. night all the plebes had a spontaneous pep rally at 10pm after study time in Tecumseh Court. It was really exciting to have 1300 guys screaming their heads off, throwing rolls of toilet paper all over the place, and carrying the football players out. We also headed over to the Superintendent's house to yell some more and listen to his pep talk. Fri night's planned pep rally in T court was even wilder—4000 midshipmen cheering for a victory over Penn State.

Of course, these rallies were in addition to all the cheering in the mess hall every meal and the posters that the Fourth Class put up in the halls last Sunday afternoon. Again backtracking, the poster my 2 roommates and I made last Monday won 2d place in our company and got us carry on till last Monday noon.

Monday night's Glee Club rehearsal was really a lot of fun. In 2 hours we read through about 20 numbers rehearsing some of them at length and just skimming over others. Most of the songs are ones used in previous years and thus familiar to the upperclassmen, but they have to learn several new ones along with us plebes. I don't have a schedule of our performances that are scheduled yet: of course, the whole schedule isn't complete yet, as the Glee Club gets many requests after the school year begins. I do know that our first performance is on 6 Oct in Washington for a Navy Ball and we have programs on 28 Oct in Chester Pa and 1 Dec in Philadelphia (where I'm not sure). The day after spring leave we go on an eight day tour of the Great Plains States—I don't know what stops that includes, but it ought to be a really terrific experience.

I was moved down to third string in football this week after a poor performance in last Saturday's scrimmage but I hope to move back up in the immediate future. I played with the 2nd string in Friday's scrimmage, however, because the first string end was injured. I think I did better this week.

I'll find out for sure tomorrow. We play NAPS (Naval Academy Prep School) this Sat. I think I'll be ready for them.

I'm not doing extremely well in academics but I'm gradually getting a little more accustomed to Academy life. Well, it's time to polish shoes and get squared away for tomorrow. I'll just pass on one more comment—some upperclass figured out that a Firstie at the Naval Academy has less freedom than a college freshman girl and a plebe has less freedom than a 2ND GRADER!!! Goodnight

John—Thanks a million to your mother for the delicious fudge; I really appreciate it (and so does my stomach) Oh yes, thank you for sending it, John. SHS must really be rolling over people in football. I hope they keep it up. You best study hard and make better grades than I am John. Thanks again for the fudge.

Barry

MON FEB 26 68 100 DAYS TILL I/C GRADUATION !!!

Tonight is the BIG NIGHT—when we lowly plebes get to switch uniforms and rank with the firsties! The month-long buildup has been a pretty busy time for me but hasn't been as trying for me as for many of my classmates. I've kept immaculately clean by taking a couple cold showers every day, built up bulging (well—sore anyway) biceps by knocking off pushups at frequent intervals, and learned my proper locker stowage backwards and forwards by restowing the heap of contents that has greeted me on several occasions. Some of my classmates have had much more intensive education, however. Several have become very good at punching a time clock, every half hour all night long, carrying two dictionaries with them everywhere, showing up for comearound in 20 pairs of sweat gear, sleeping braced up on the bed springs in full dress blue, smoking cigars under an inverted waste can (I got some experience here) and so on. TONIGHT THE TABLES ARE TURNED!!! I'm just going to more or less play games with my firstie since he hasn't been too tough on me but more than a few first class are going to suffer tonight. In case I didn't mention it, my firstie did take me off training tables for the last two weeks so I could brace up at his company table. My T-table was cut (end of season) last Sat., so I'll be back on company tables for good.

The basketball season ended Sat night with Navy's loss to Army; spring football starts a week from today and goes for a month. I'm not in the best shape for football right now but I am looking forward to it (and will be even more if I can get caught up on some much needed sleep)

The Glee Club performance at Bethel Temple (Synagogue) in Baltimore was another tremendous experience! The audience (congregation) was the warmest and most responsive we've had (throughout the entire 3 hour program). Their own Cantor Hammerman did about half of the performance and the Glee Club and Blue Buoys (folk duet in the Glee Club—guitar and brass violin) did the rest plus a couple of joint numbers. The Blue Buoys did an excellent job—They're really good.

In addition to serving a delicious meal before the concert, their congregation held a champagne ball afterward. Through a misunderstanding, there was a shortage of girls, however, so most of the (mids) midshipmen just enjoyed the music, fellowship, and of course champagne. I got my kicks watching everybody else and just sticking with my classmates. I tasted the "joy juice" and then drank water the rest of the night. (It tasted bitter and totally disagreed with me)

However, most of the others liked it, and some a little too much. All in all the trip was really great. Back to the books.

SAT NIGHT MARCH 2 1968

Finally it's Sat night; thank goodness this week is over! The past 5 days have been physically trying ones for this plebe. After 100th night, I started going on all calls (every comearound) to a second class who thinks I haven't been putting out enough; he managed to give my young body some pretty good workouts. Since this was the first week of [the] academic year that I haven't been participating in plebe athletics, I had to go to evening comearounds (30 minutes) as well as morning sessions. I also had to run off 4 hours of Extra Duty—a plebe gets one hour extra duty for every 5 demerits—that I have been deferring because of athletics. And I had a PMW (Plebe Morning Workout—30 minutes) to get out of the way. On Wed. I spent 3 hours doing physical exercise for misdemeanors—now you know where my time goes (that is very unusual however, I've never been run more than an hour any other day and even that is uncommon) I wouldn't have minded the additional exercise so much if I hadn't been tired and sick the whole week, pero asi es la vida (such is life)

HUNDREDTH NIGHT was something else!!! We really had a blast—I can understand why my firstie was worried that I'd become drunk with power that night. I wasn't too hard on him, but I did make him do most of the stuff that he'd made me do during the previous four weeks. Evening meal in the mess hall was one big "food free for all" Everybody was pouring pitchers of tea on everybody else. Giving shampoos with green beans, throwing sugar, bread, and anything that would make a mess, and so on. By the end of the "meal" the mess hall was totally gross; we plebes (the real ones) stayed after and helped clean up. The whole thing was a little wilder than I expected, but it was really great fun (personally I think we ought to do it every week) There were some pretty worn out firsties the next day.

Last night I had the skeleton watch at main office from midnight to 4 a.m. went to sleep for 3½ hours, and then stood again from 8:30 a.m. till noon. I slept a couple of hours this afternoon and am planning to hit the pad early tonight.

SPRING FOOTBALL starts Monday. I'm not in the best condition right now, but there's no such thing as an "out of shape plebe" My body is pretty worn down right now but maybe I'll be able to get the needed recovery this weekend.

We have our 4th teafight tomorrow; I can't get too excited about it, but it is a change of pace and always gives us plebes a lot to talk about.

Well, it's approaching my padtime and the end of the page is closing in on me. I surely hope Shelbyville was able to come out of the regional victorious tonight. Goodnight!

John—You don't have to look at Miss Chenoweth—just listen to her. She's a good teacher.

Barry

SAT NIGHT APRIL 6 1968

Yes, I'm spending Sat night in the usual way—a quiet evening at home?. I'm really beat and sleepy (as always) but I HAVE to go to another tea fight tomorrow, so I want to get the SHAMBACH WEEKLY (Annapolis Edition) in print. I wasn't supposed to have to go to this tea fight (we allegedly are required to attend 4 of 6 and I got roped into the first 4) but somebody goofed and invited too many babes so all of us have to go. Personally, I'd rather spend tomorrow afternoon in the pad writing letters (but nobody asked me)

We had our final football scrimmage of the spring season today in the form of a game between the first team (offense and defense) against the rest of the squad. I've been playing second string all week and so got to play a little over half today. I really blew a few plays (that went for long yardage) because of a mix up in assignments (I was wrong)—I wish I could say other than that I did great, but I didn't, so I'll just say I didn't have a real good day. The rest of the week went okay football wise.

Now that football's over I get to go back to company tables (to my firstie's table that is) and I get to "go around" 3 times a day instead of just twice (Oh yes—I also get to MARCH again—what fun?!) I've been performing well for my firstie the last 2 weeks; but he's dedicated to the job of making a real plebe out of me. Oh well—I have had it better than a lot of my classmates all year, so I hope to get rested up and study quite a bit more (even though I'll have a few more professional activities.) I've had trouble studying again this week just because I've been plumb tuckered out.

Last week—Sun night that is—the Naval Academy Christian Association (NACA) sponsored the NEW FOLK here. The NEW FOLK is a terrific folk-singing group made up of 5 boys and 4 girls—all in college; more importantly, however, their program was designed to bring Christ into the lives of the college-student (midshipman in our case) audience. After presenting several excellent and original numbers, three of the group told of their personal experience of accepting Christ as Savior and the joy of salvation he brings. After this part of the program, they passed out cards for comments on the performance and for those who would be interested in getting into a Bible study group and /or would like materials on Christian maturity. The members of the group stayed around afterwards to talk to individuals and small groups and to truly witness for Christ. What made the program so effective was that these young adults were the same age as the midshipmen and had quite a bit in common. The group is sponsored by Campus Crusade for Christ International and was winding up a week long tour of major college campuses across the nation. As you have probably noticed, this experience had quite a profound effect on me. I received the booklet "Ten Basic Steps to Christian Maturity" and other materials from the Campus Crusade . . . just the other day and am finding the reading/study very interesting, stimulating and challenging.

I just realized that this is the first 2 page letter I've written since plebe summer—which come to think of it isn't really earth-shattering but—just a thought.

The Academy has been guarded by Marines for the last two days and all upperclass liberty outside the 7 mile limit has been cancelled for this weekend. Right now the "domestic tranquility of the nation" is really coming apart at the seams, it seems; no, I don't think the shooting of Dr. King was too smart an idea—in fact, it was pretty idiotic and senseless if you ask me.

Before that last paragraph I was going to try to make you believe my typing is improving (would you believe a little bit?) But now I see that I have too many errors to stand on.

As my chemistry prof says before every chem lab, "Good luck and the Lord be with you" (I could use a little more luck on these labs)

Mon Morning

John

Would you believe last week's newsletter? I had an enjoyable visit with my parents and relatives yesterday—their visit made my Easter a little more special. I'm glad you're enjoying yourself at Wabash—good luck on the canoe trip. Gotta hit the books!

Barry

P.S. No newsletter this week—not much news.

Glossary

Never stagnant, Naval Academy language can be hard to pin down. The following terms appear in the letters in this book. The definitions included here may prove helpful to readers. In addition to the glossaries in *Reef Points* and *The Lucky Bag,* definitions of USNA slang can be found in *Good Gouge: An Investigation into the Origins of Naval Academy Slang,* by Professor Michael Parker and his students. Also of interest is a thin little book called *The Whichness of What.* All these sources are available in the Special Collections Section of the Nimitz Library at the U.S. Naval Academy.

bilge: to fail an examination; to make another look bad; to fail out of the academy

bone: to study

brace up: to stand erect; to rotate the hips, chest out, chin in

bull: any humanities subject; English

carry on: to have rules relaxed, for example, to be granted a privilege after a sports victory

Com: commandant of midshipmen

Crabtown: Annapolis

dago: any romance language

date: the date of a midshipman's warrant; in the early years, students were grouped by the "date," not year of graduation

dope: the latest information

firsties: college seniors; also known as First Class

French out: to leave the academy without permission

fry: to assign demerits; to place on the daily conduct report

gouge: a list of necessary facts; essential information; to cheat

haze: to subject to cruel horseplay; to bully or maltreat underclassmen

list: sick or excused list

no more rivers: a river is a term examination; after four years, there are no more rivers

O.A.O.: one and only (girl)

O.C.: officer in charge

O.D.: officer of the day

pap: a conduct report; to inflict demerits

plebe: college freshman; also known as Fourth Class

rate: to be entitled to; to rate a privilege is to be entitled to that privilege

reform: when the entire student body returns after a break, the brigade is said to reform

Reina Mercedes: the detention ship; earlier the *Santee* served this purpose

rhino: complaint sessions

run: to haze, usually in its milder forms

Second Class: college junior

skinny: physics, chemistry

spoon: to befriend an underclassman; to address an underclassman, especially a plebe, by his first name

stand: to hold a class rank, as in *he stood sixth in his class*

star: to have an academic average of 3.4; one who stars

steam: thermodynamics; marine engineering

steerage: midshipman snack bar

Supe: superintendent of U.S. Naval Academy

teafight: a social function; a dance

tree: weekly listing of those who are academically deficient

unsat: academically deficient

velvet: academic surplus above 2.5, carried over from month to month

weak squad: those deficient in strength tests or gymnasium requirements

Yard: academy grounds

youngster: college sophomore; second year midshipman

Index

About the Editor

As an English professor and director of the Masqueraders at the United States Naval Academy, Anne Marie Drew's primary research area is theater history. She is the recipient of various research grants and has worked with primary sources at the Covent Garden Theater Museum, the Victoria and Albert Museum, the Samuel Beckett Archives at the University of Reading, and the Shakespeare Centre Library at Stratford-upon-Avon. She has also worked extensively with the collection at the Folger Shakespeare Library and the Stratford Festival Archives.

In 1990, the National Endowment for the Humanities and the Indiana Humanities Council awarded her a grant to produce, direct, and write a radio program, *Legends and Letters.* The program, a blend of dramatic readings and music, incorporated the letters and writings of people as diverse as Henry VIII and American slaves.

In addition to many scholarly articles and reviews, her publication credits include a number of books. In addition, she regularly writes for various magazines and newspapers.

THE NAVAL INSTITUTE PRESS is the book-publishing arm of the U.S. Naval Institute, a private, nonprofit, membership society for sea service professionals and others who share an interest in naval and maritime affairs. Established in 1873 at the U.S. Naval Academy in Annapolis, Maryland, where its offices remain today, the Naval Institute has members worldwide.

Members of the Naval Institute support the education programs of the society and receive the influential monthly magazine *Proceedings* and discounts on fine nautical prints and on ship and aircraft photos. They also have access to the transcripts of the Institute's Oral History Program and get discounted admission to any of the Institute-sponsored seminars offered around the country.

The Naval Institute also publishes *Naval History* magazine. This colorful bimonthly is filled with entertaining and thought-provoking articles, first-person reminiscences, and dramatic art and photography. Members receive a discount on *Naval History* subscriptions.

The Naval Institute's book-publishing program, begun in 1898 with basic guides to naval practices, has broadened its scope in recent years to include books of more general interest. Now the Naval Institute Press publishes about 100 titles each year, ranging from how-to books on boating and navigation to battle histories, biographies, ship and aircraft guides, and novels. Institute members receive discounts of 20 to 50 percent on the Press's nearly 600 books in print.

Full-time students are eligible for special half-price membership rates. Life memberships are also available.

For a free catalog describing Naval Institute Press books currently available, and for further information about subscribing to *Naval History* magazine or about joining the U.S. Naval Institute, please write to:

Membership Department
U.S. NAVAL INSTITUTE
118 Maryland Avenue
Annapolis, MD 21402-5035
Telephone: (800) 233-8764
Fax: (410) 269-7940
Web address: www.usni.org